COLORING BOOKS FOR ADULTS

Beautiful Birds

Adult Coloring Book with Stress Relieving Bird Designs

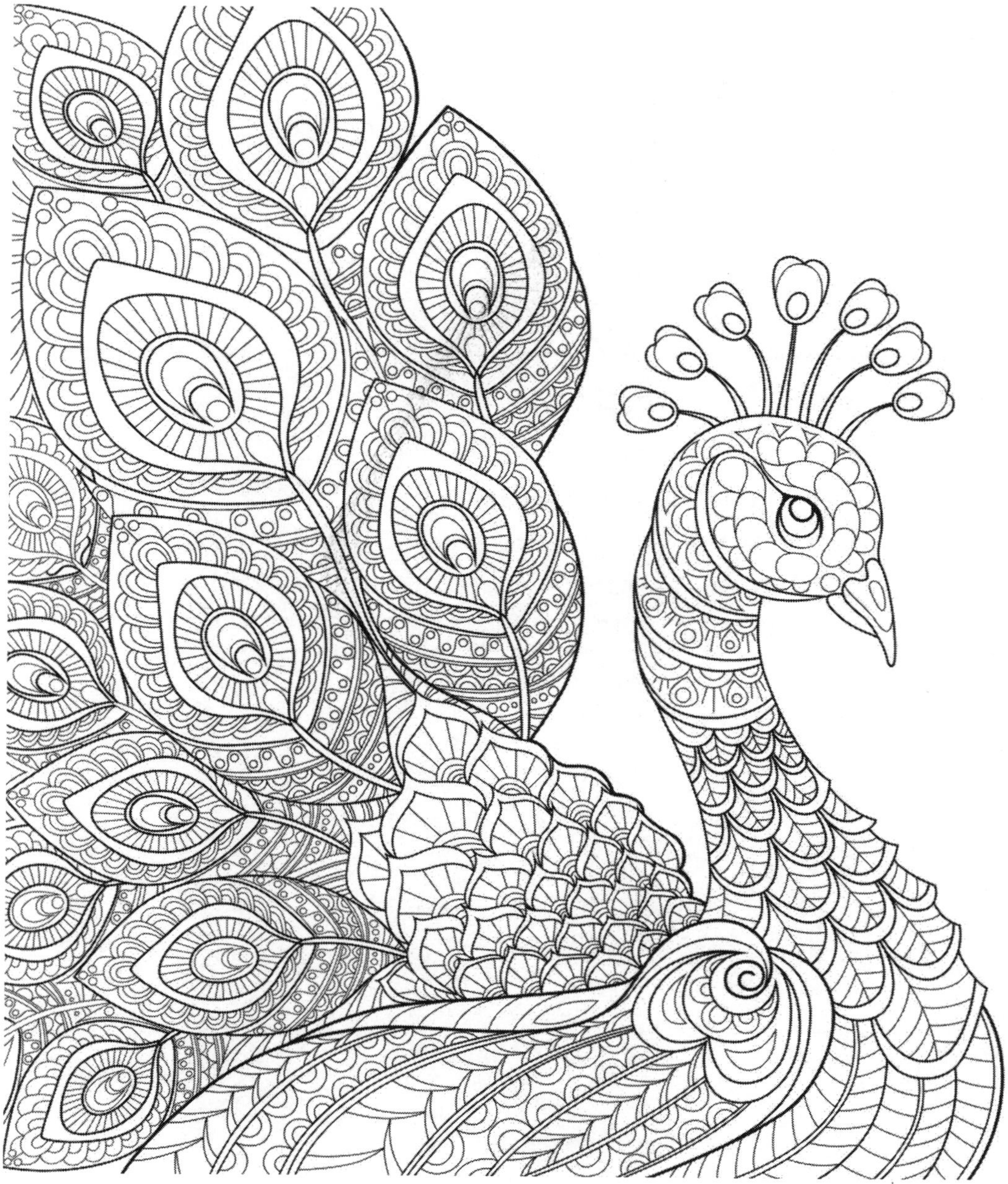

MantraCraft

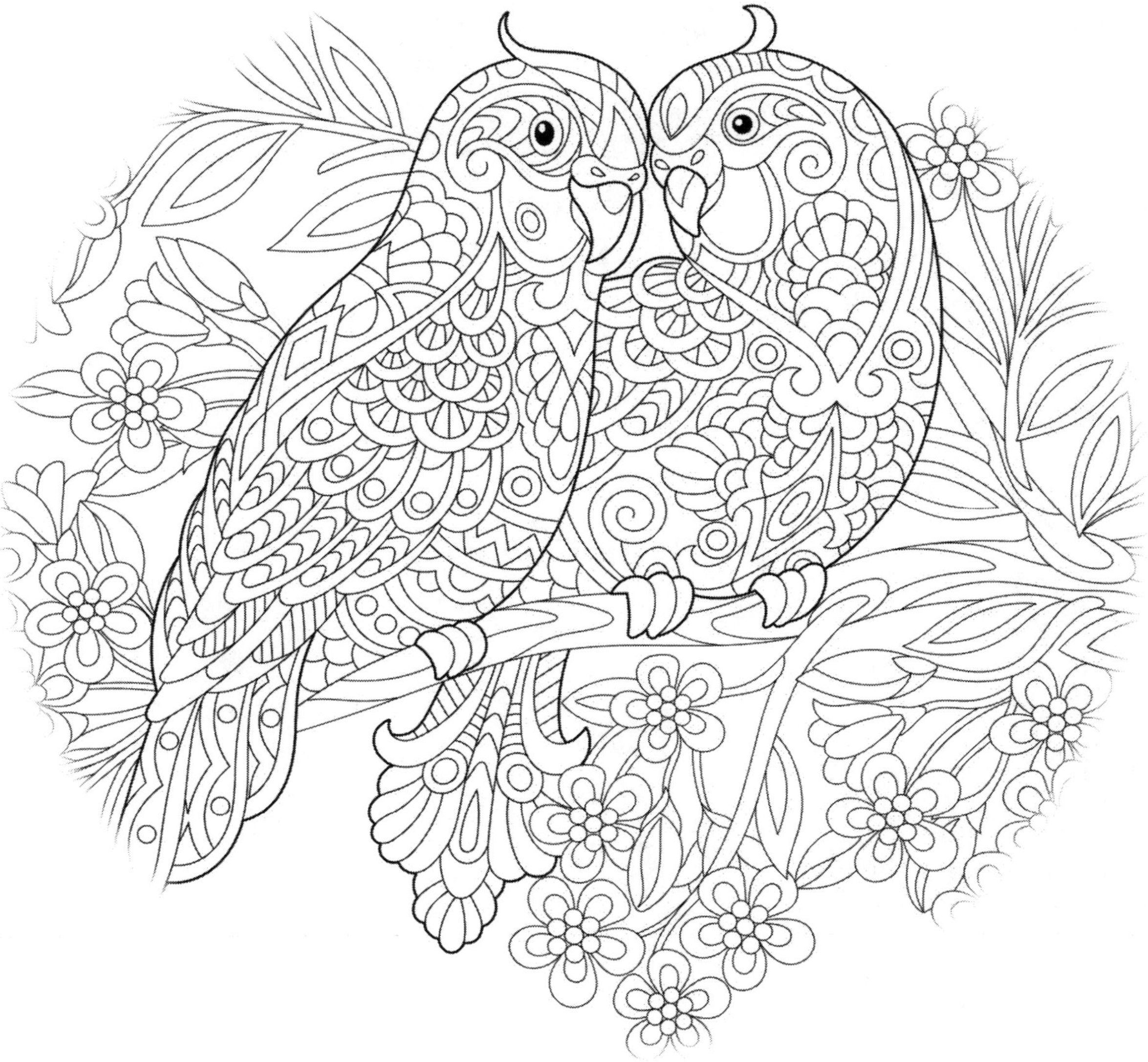

This Beautiful Birds Coloring Book
belongs to:

Color Test Page

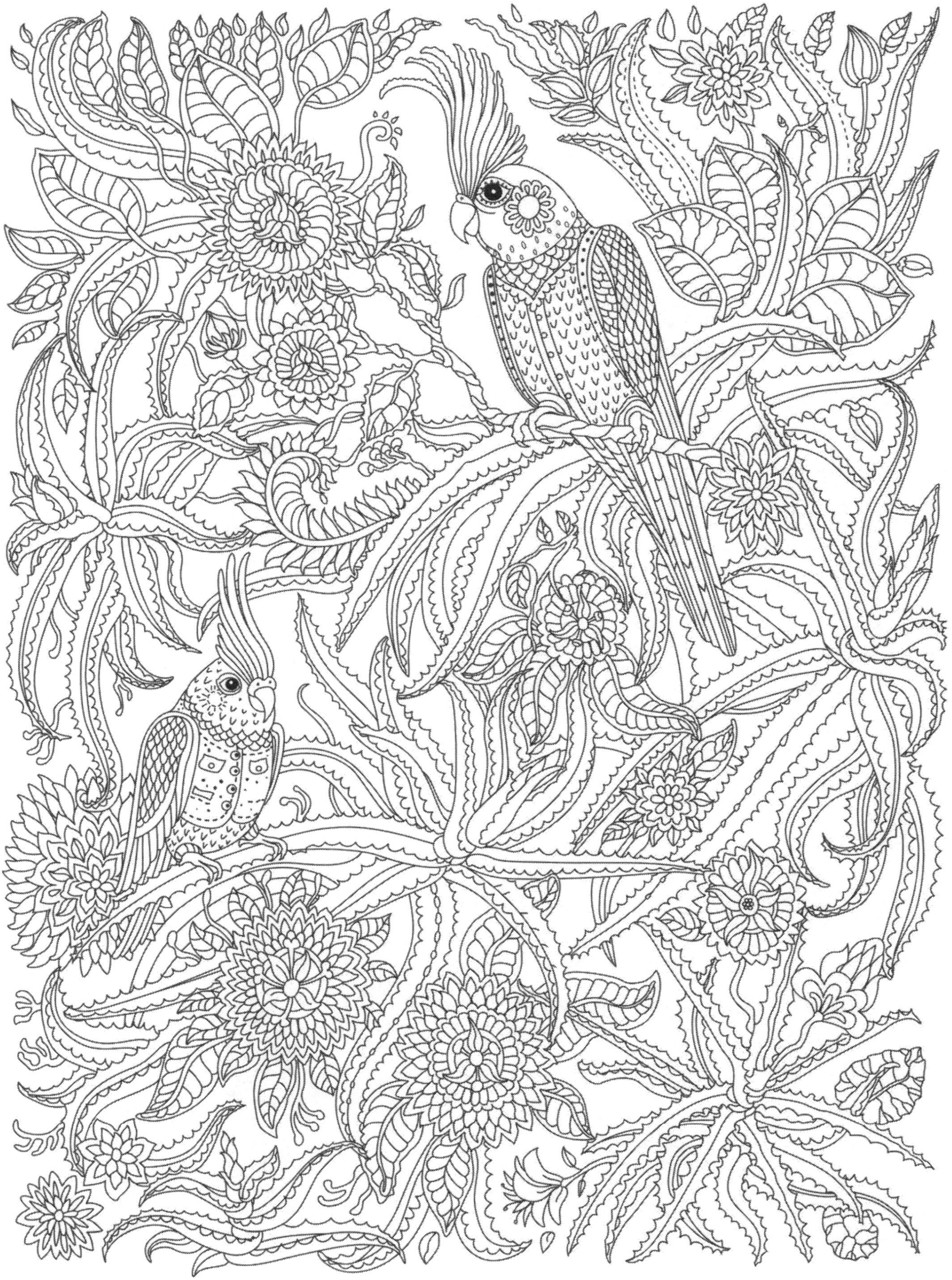

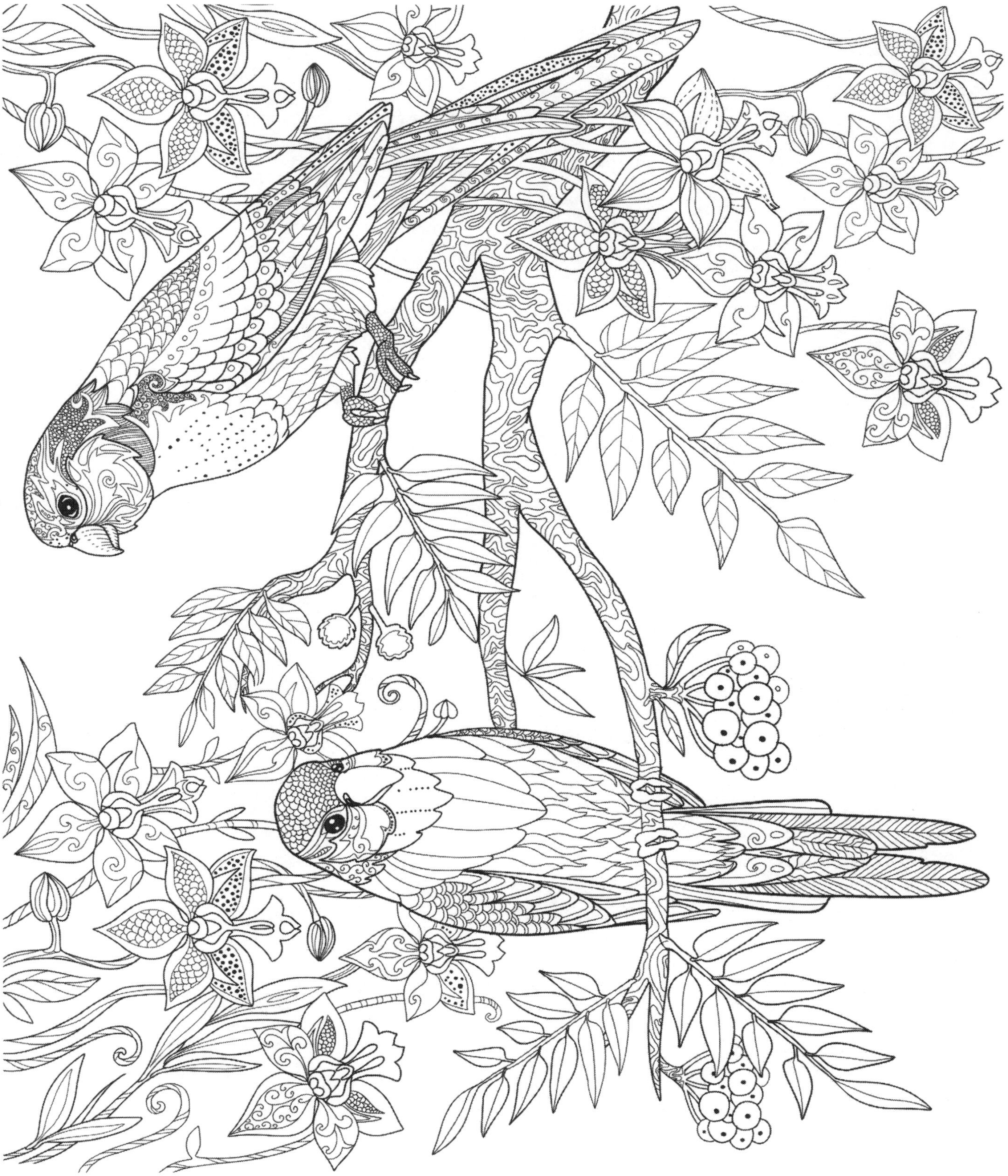

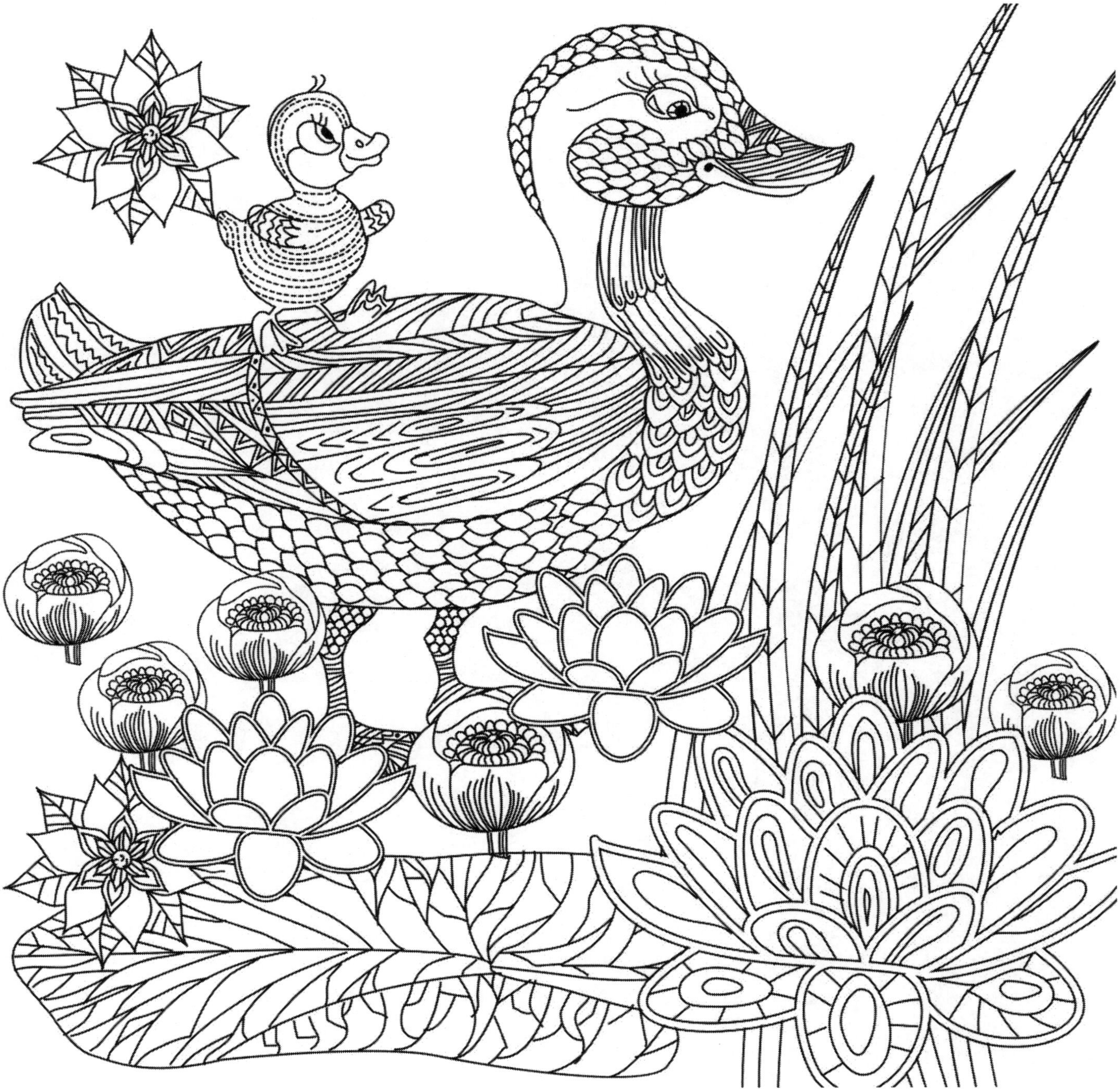

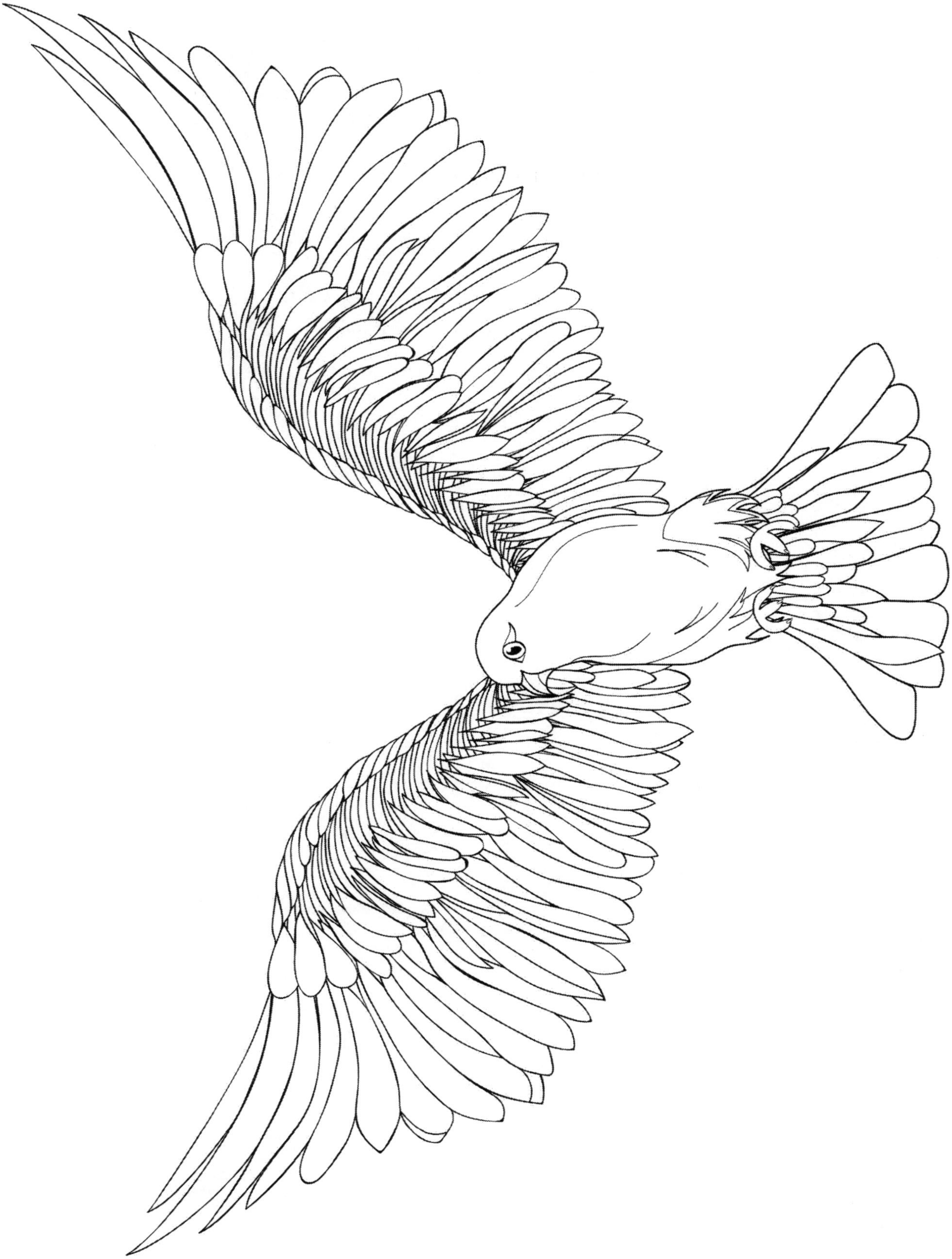

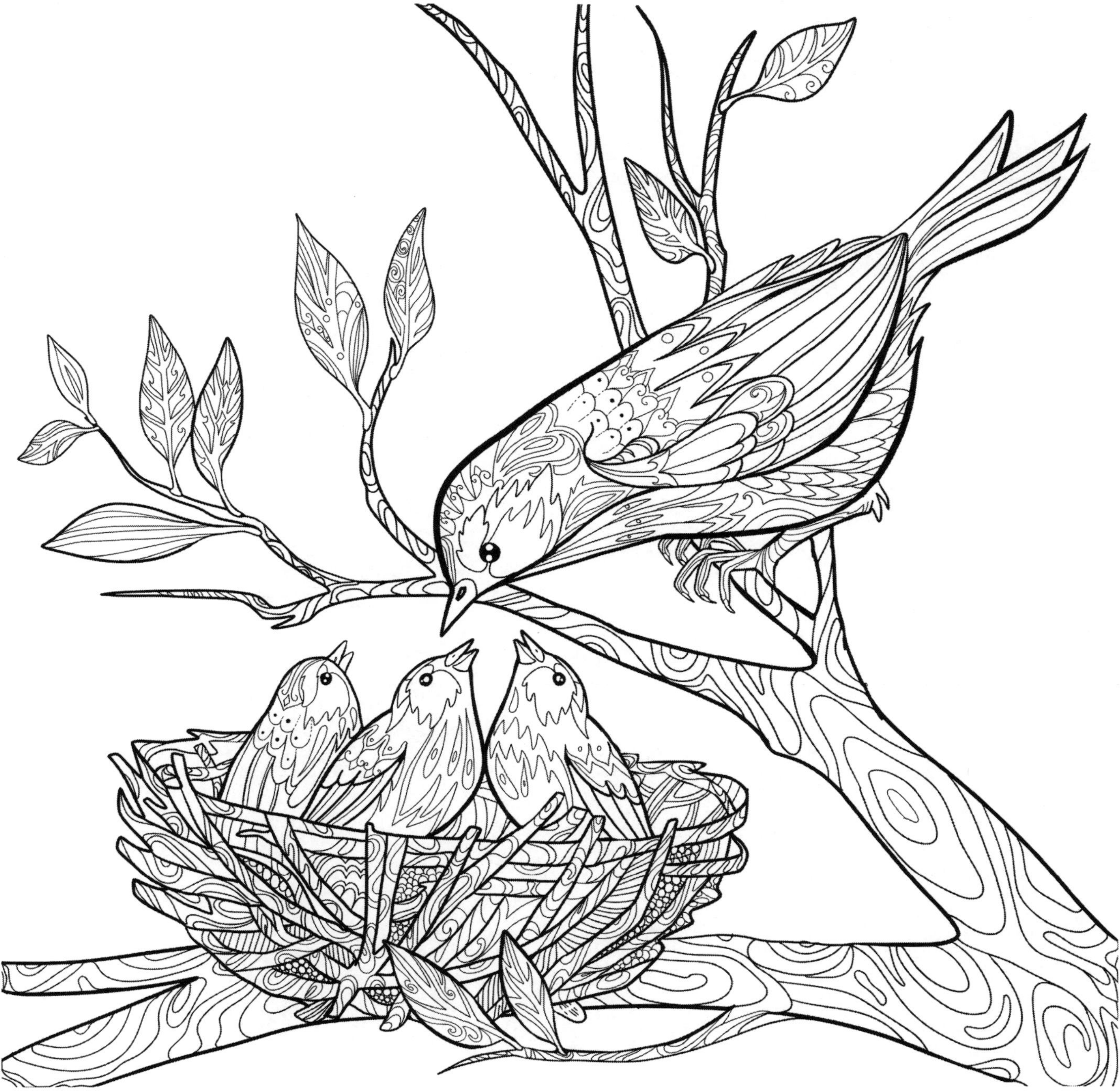

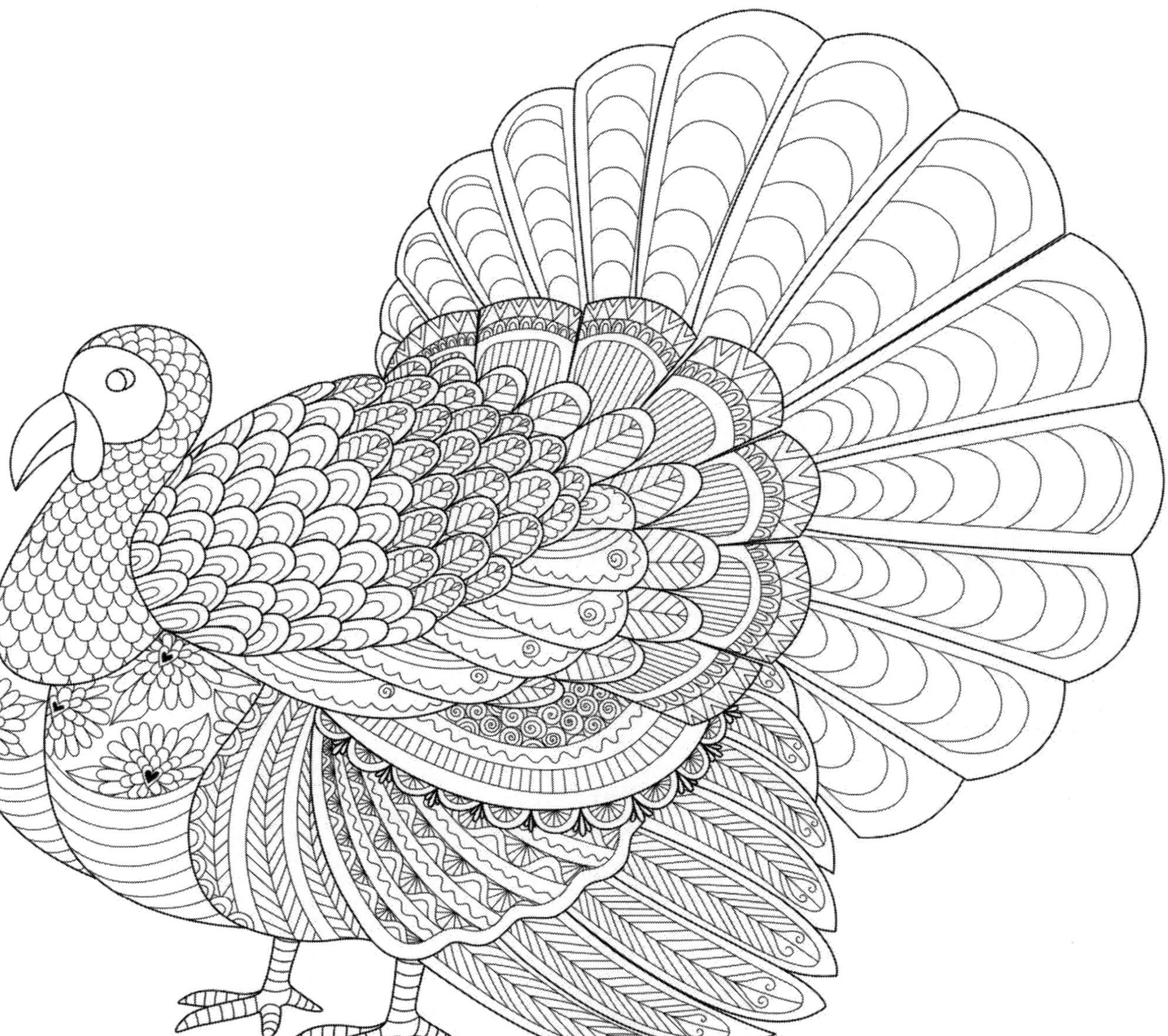

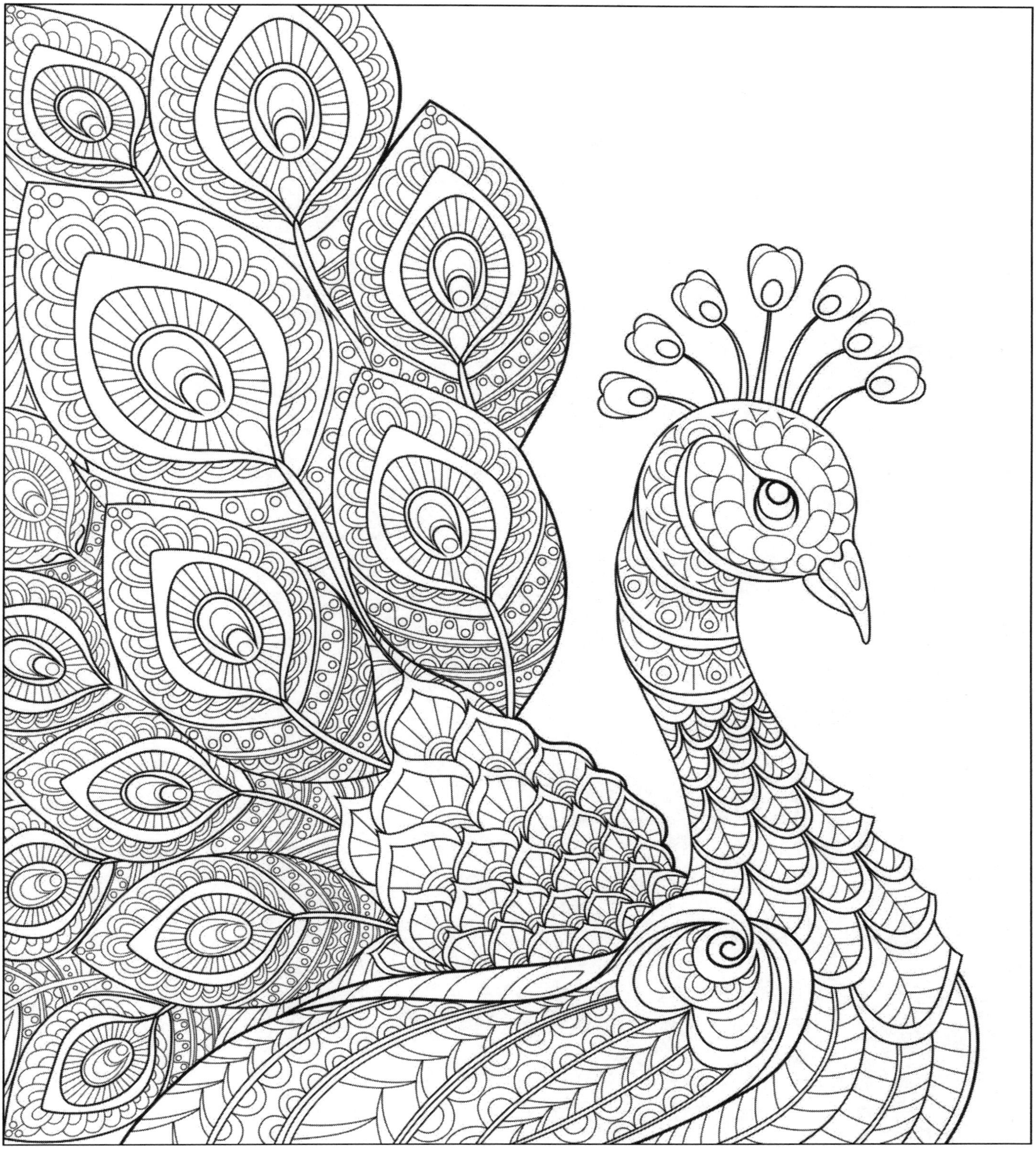

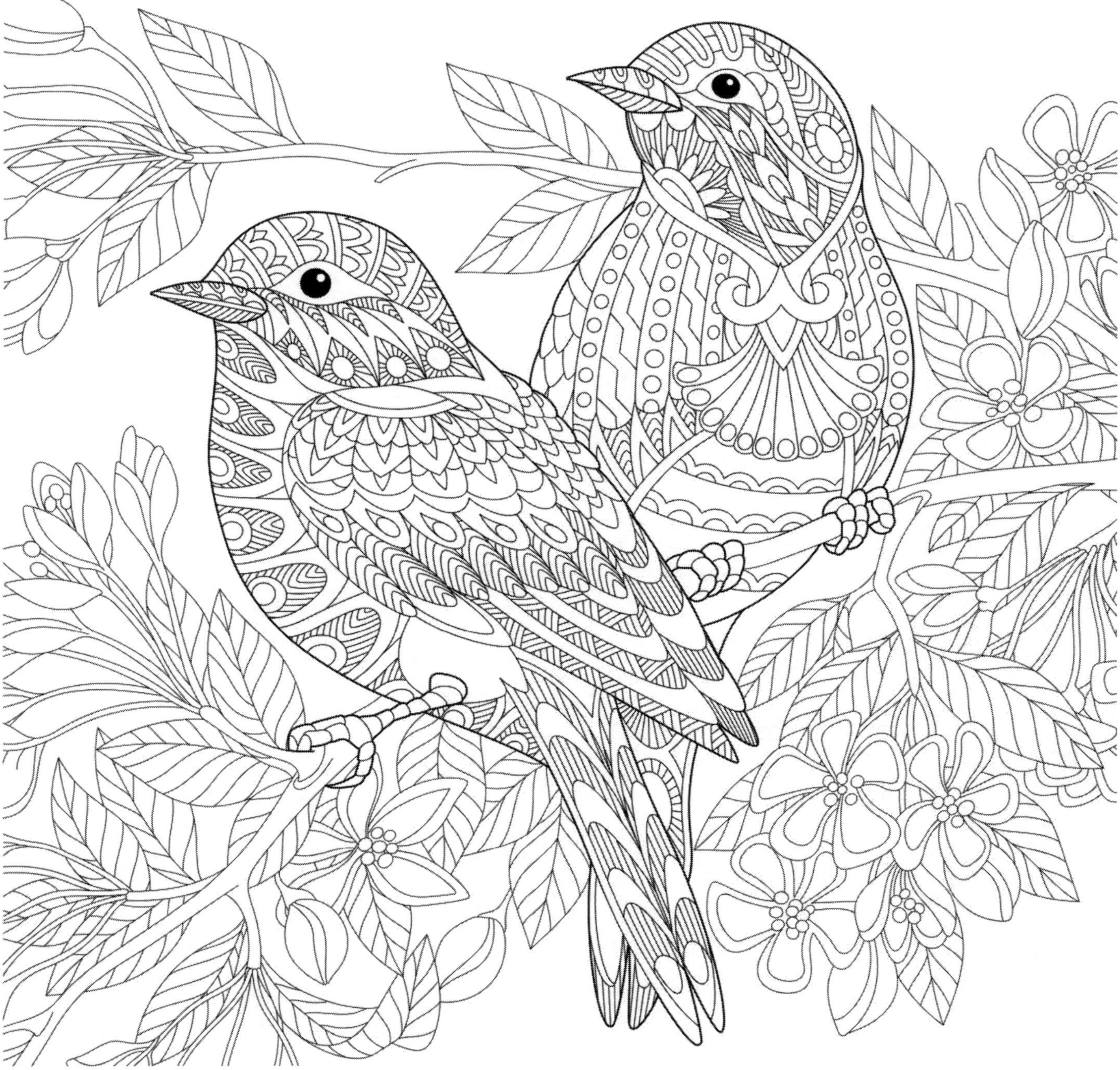

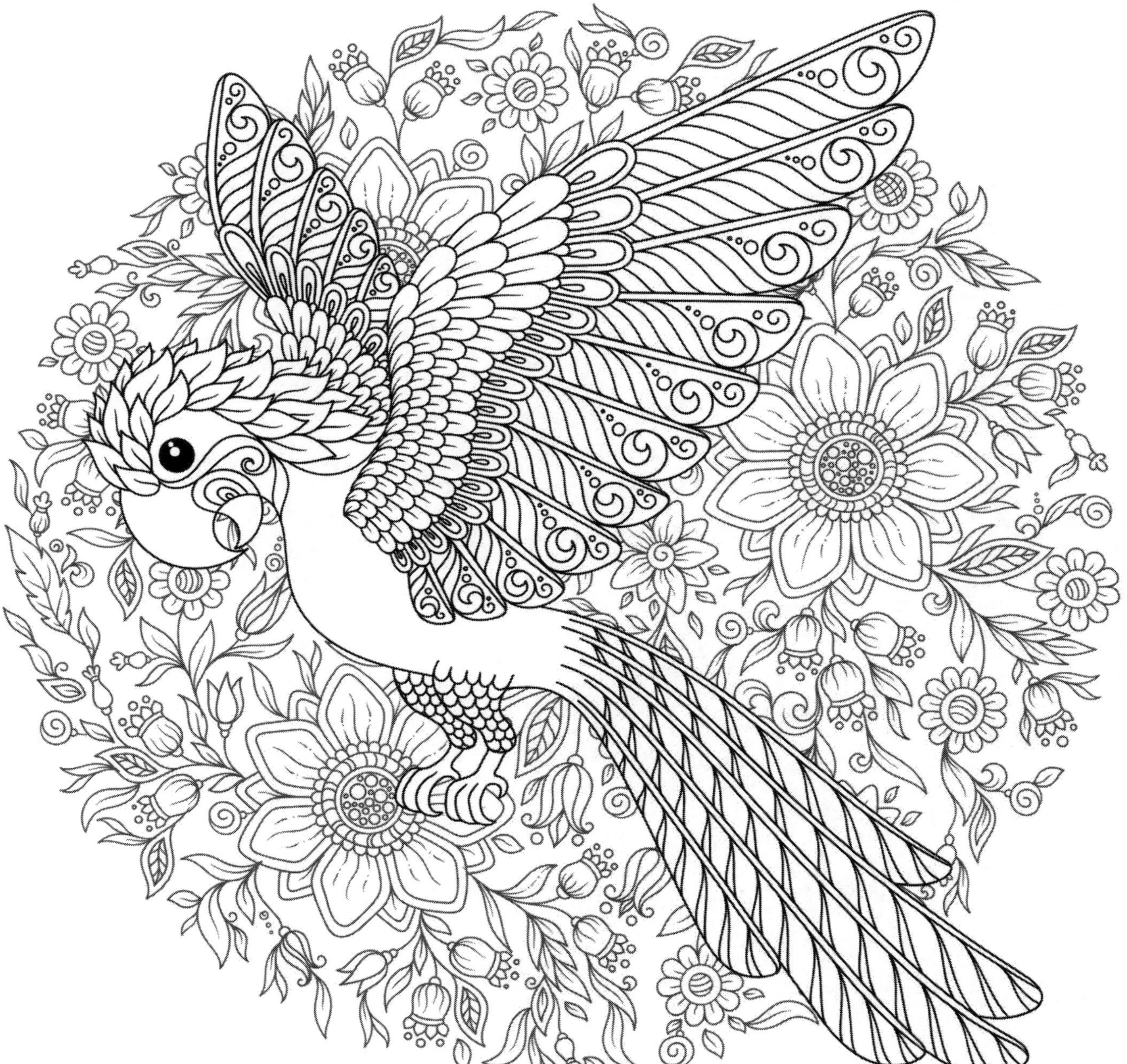

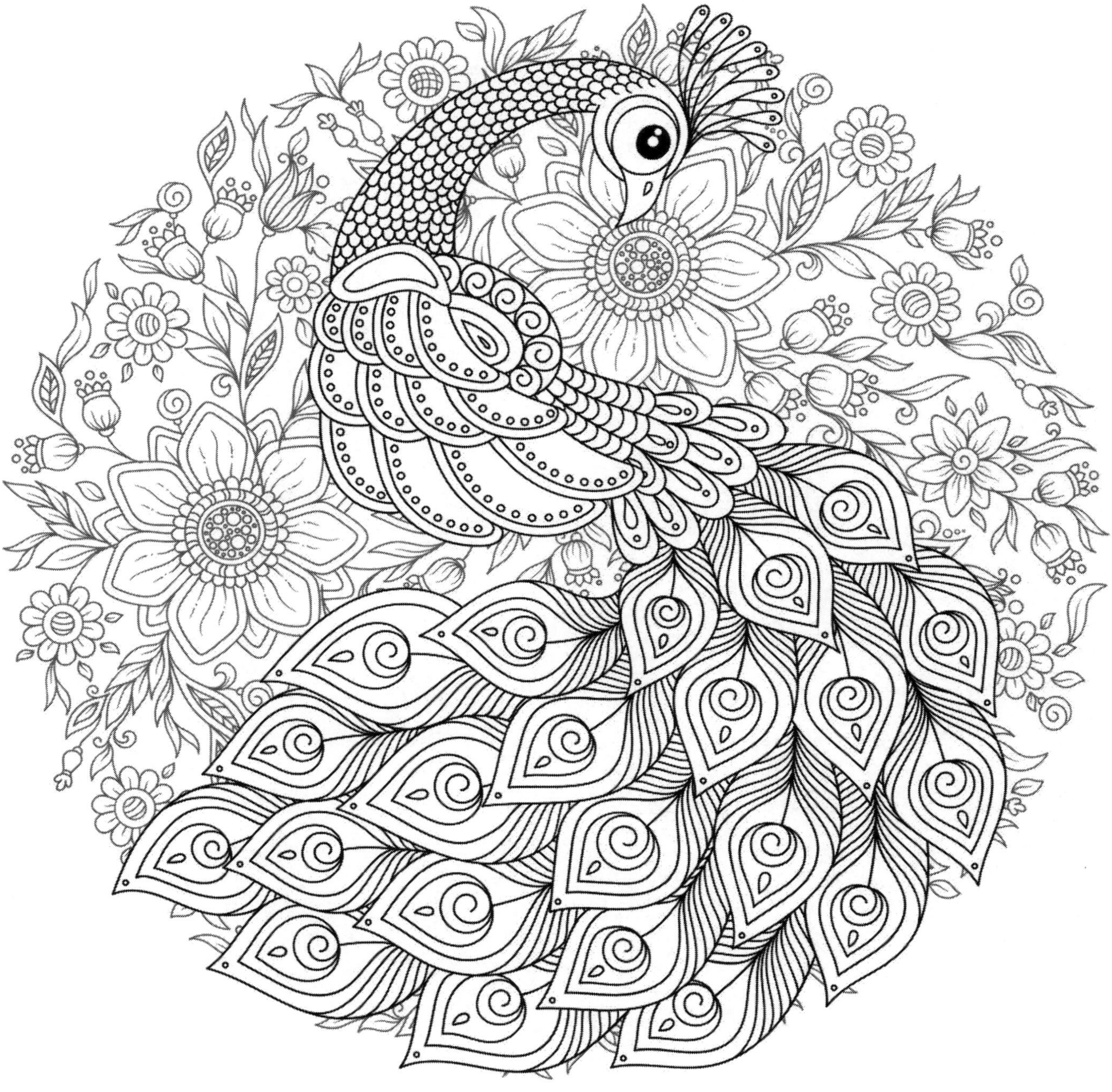

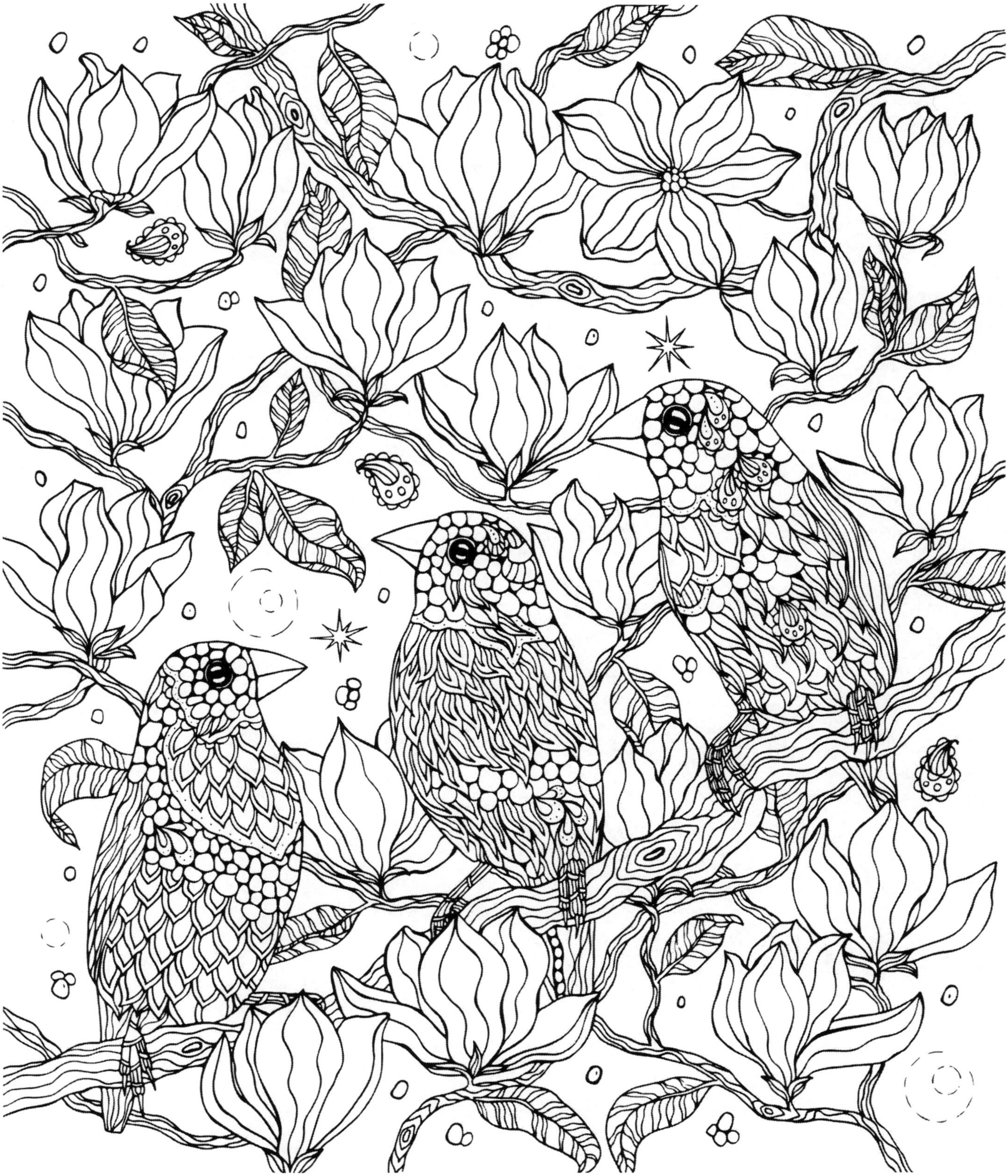

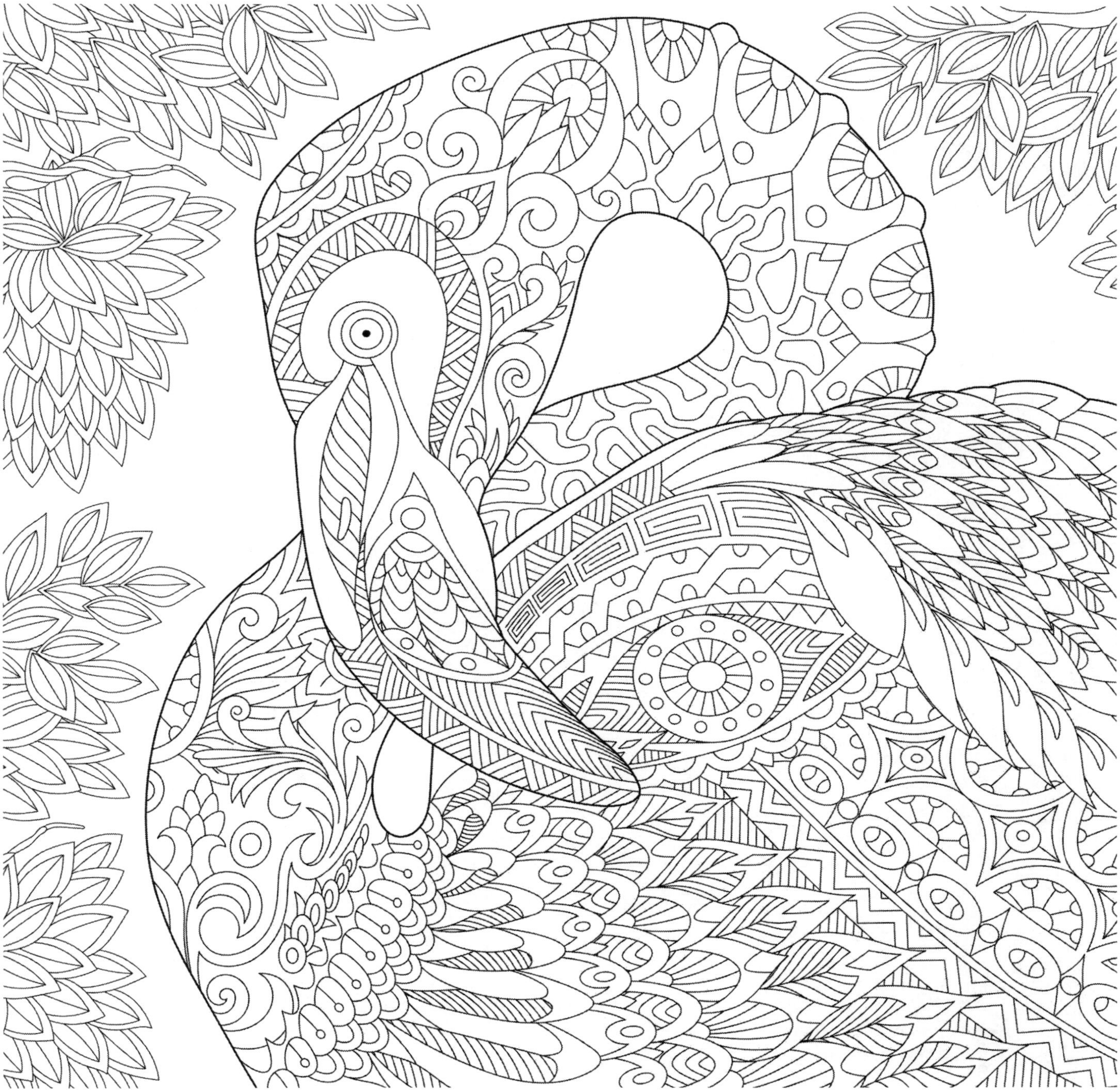

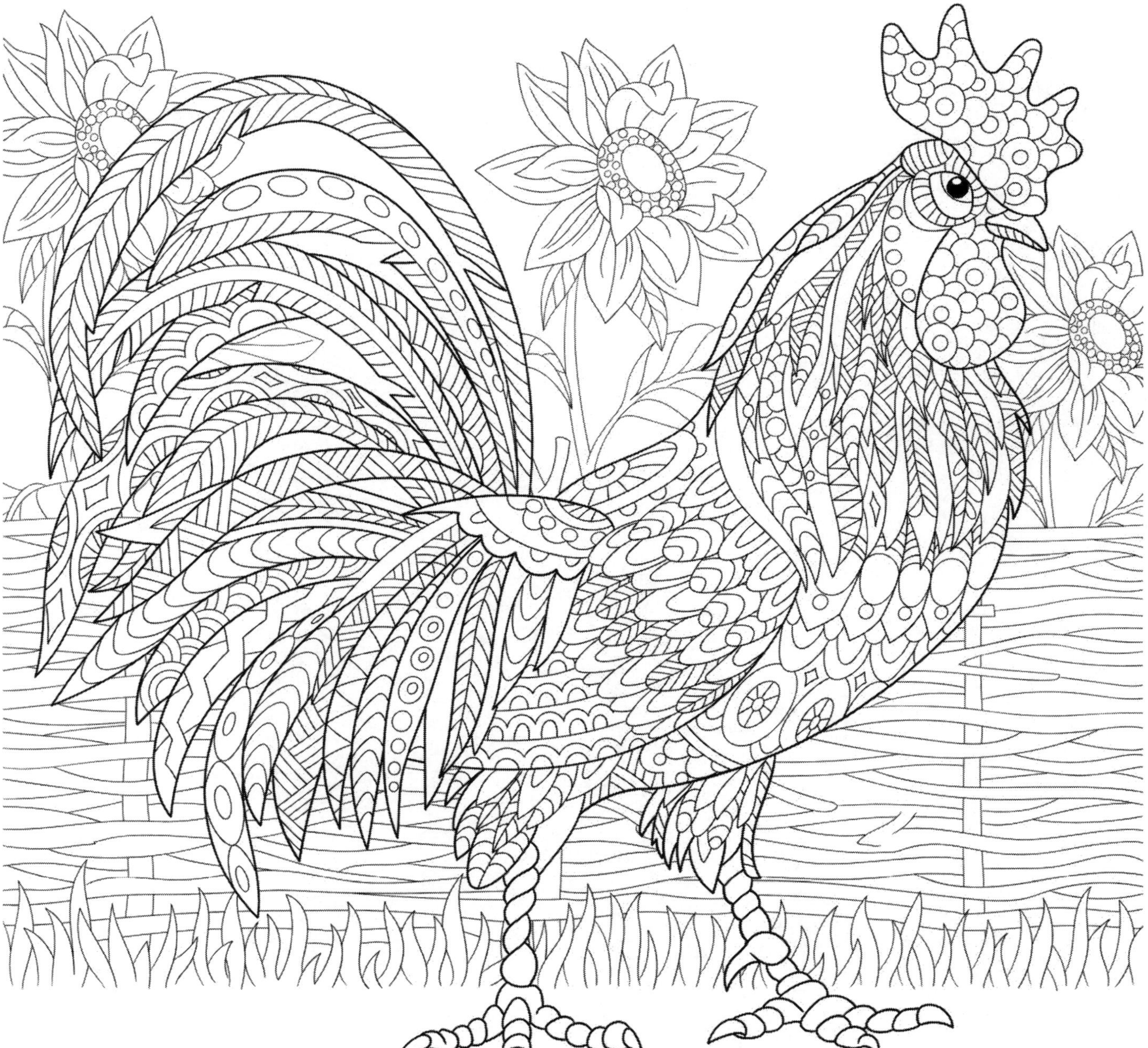

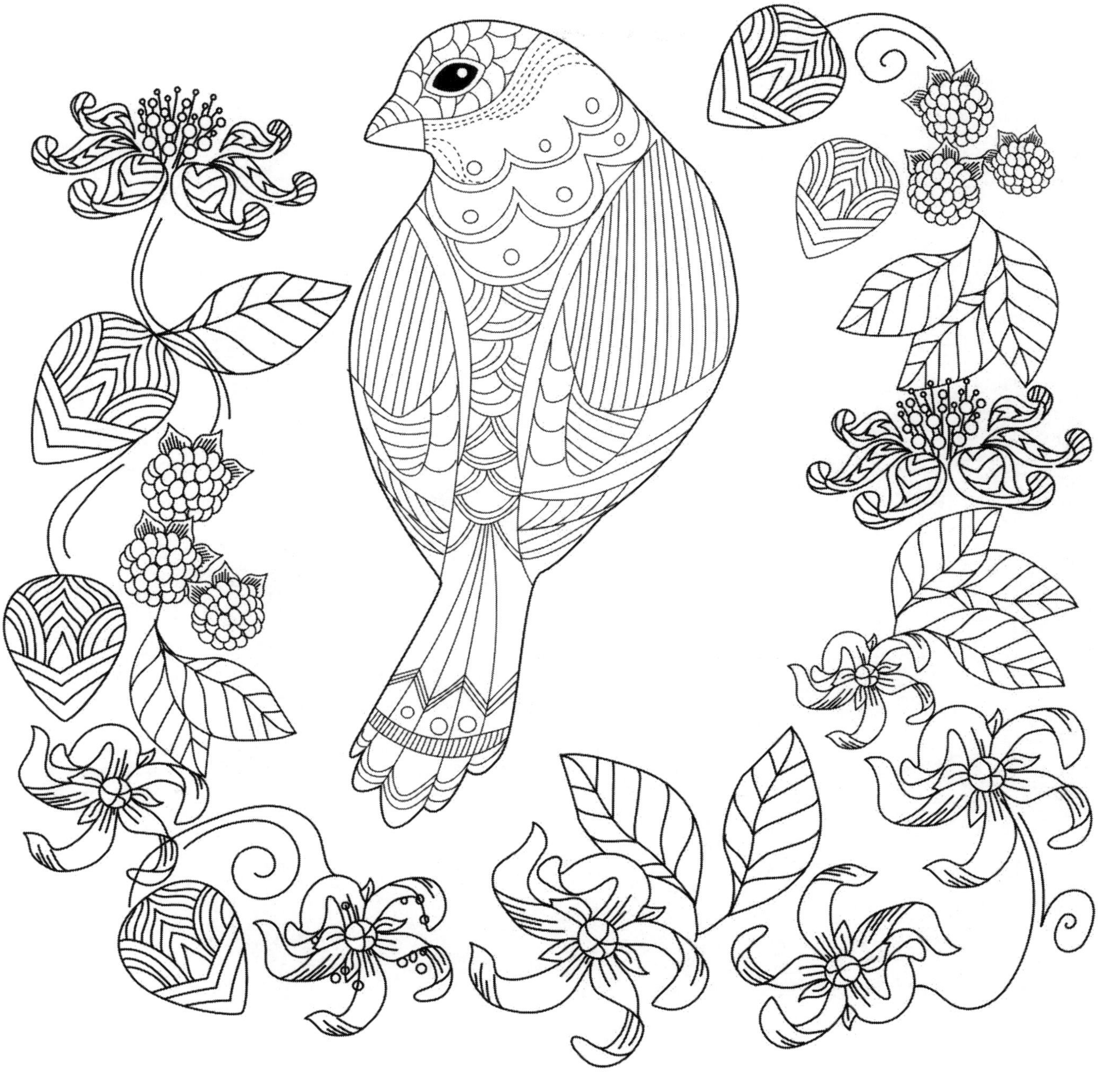

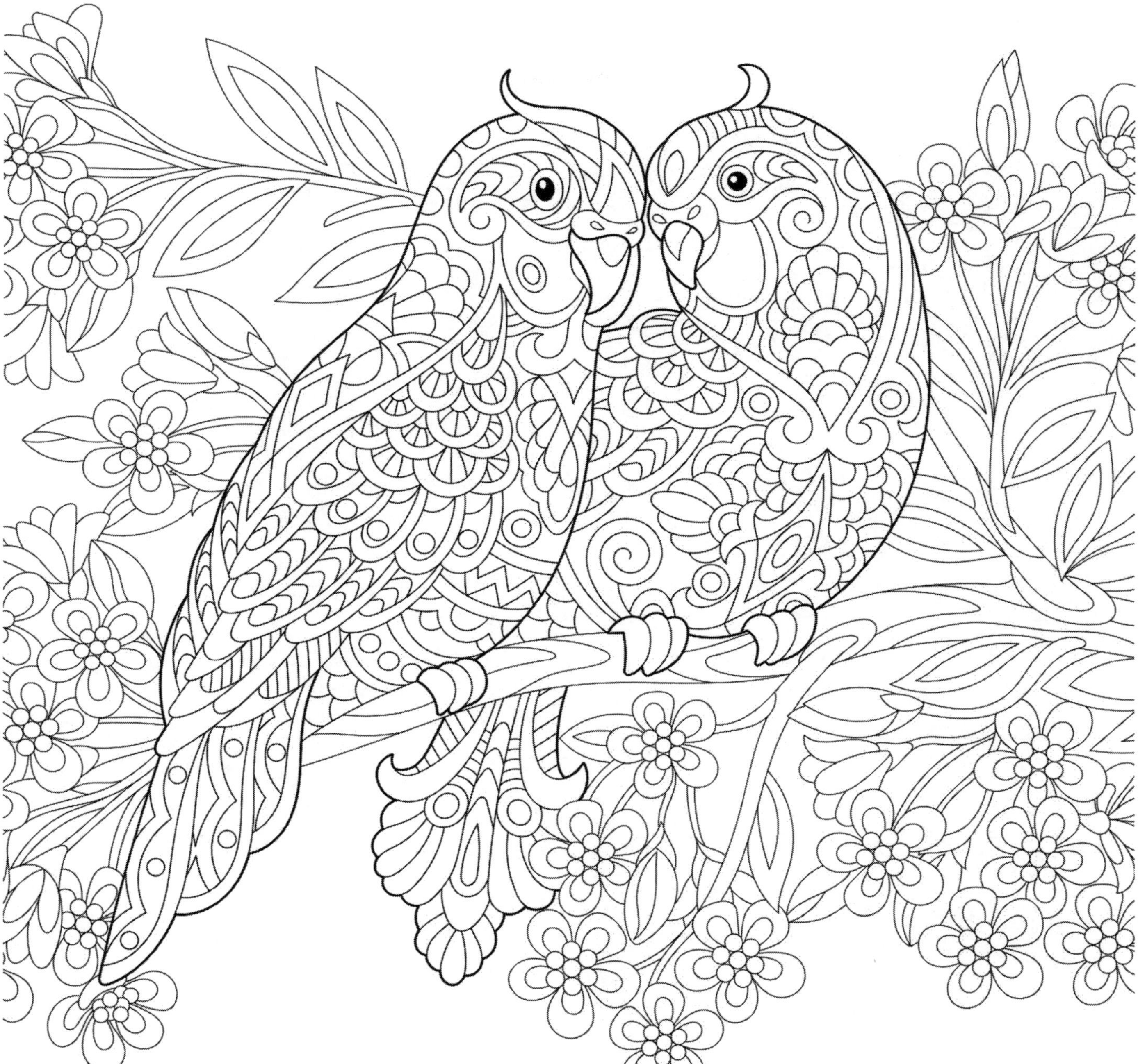

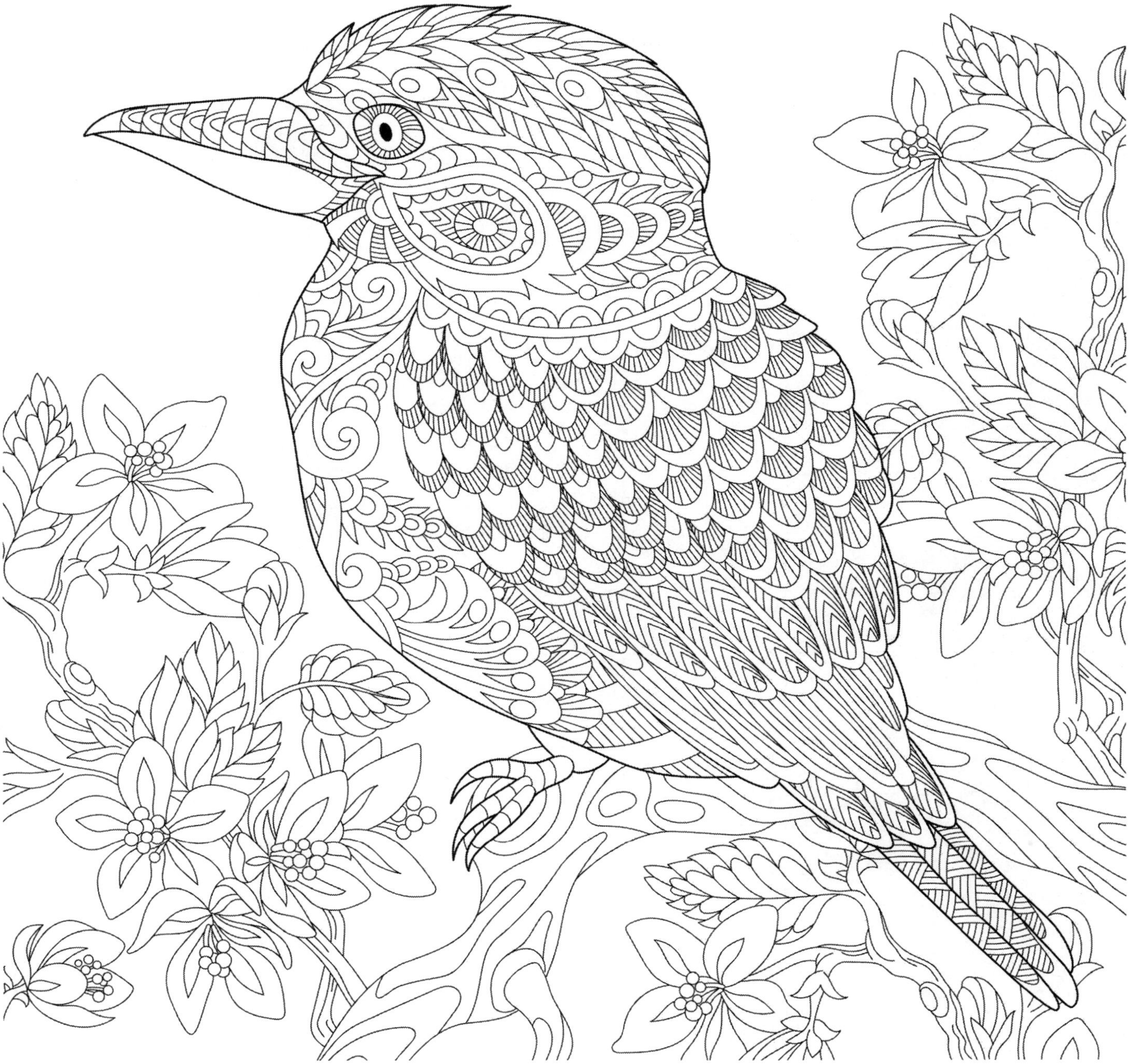

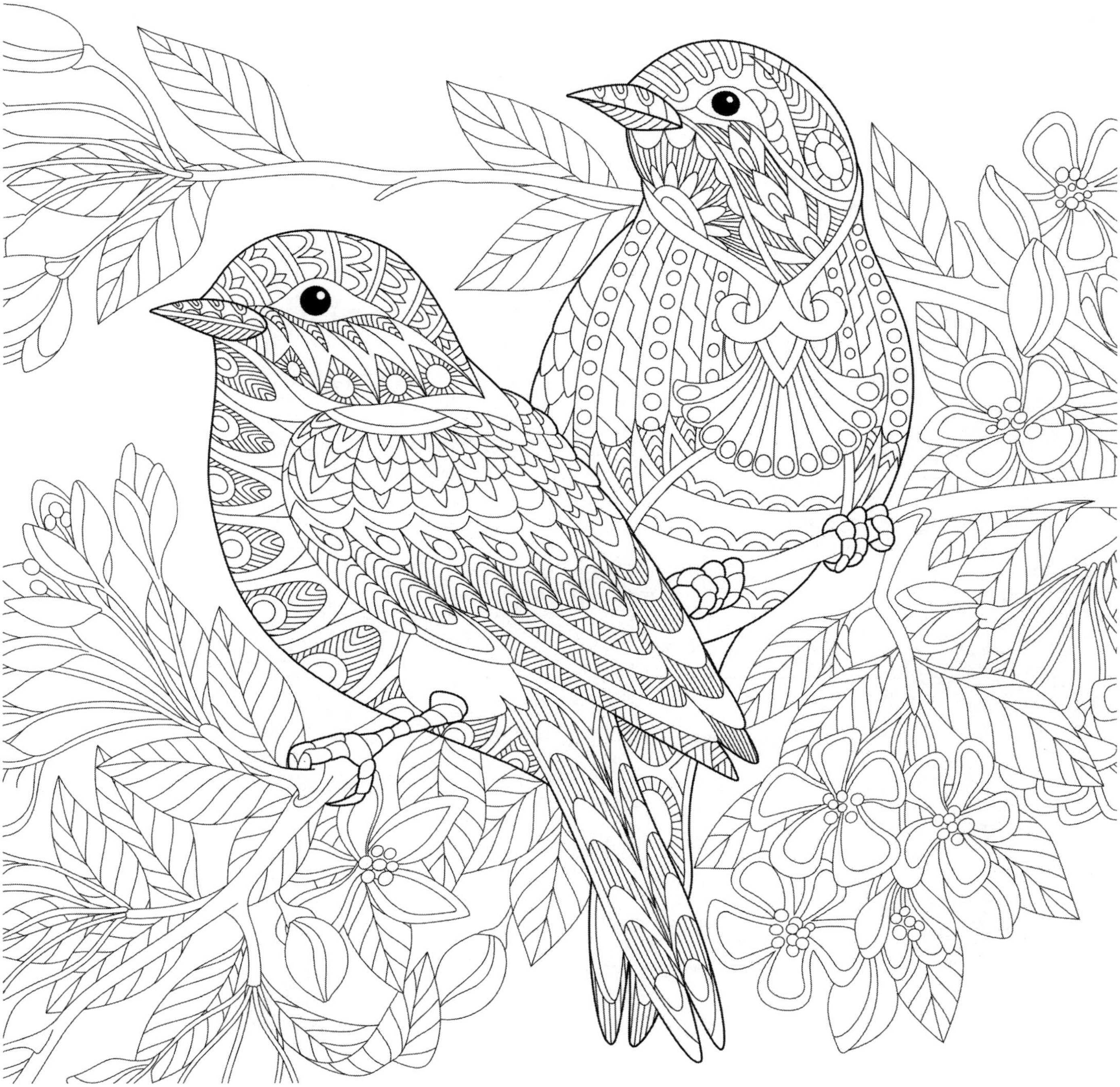

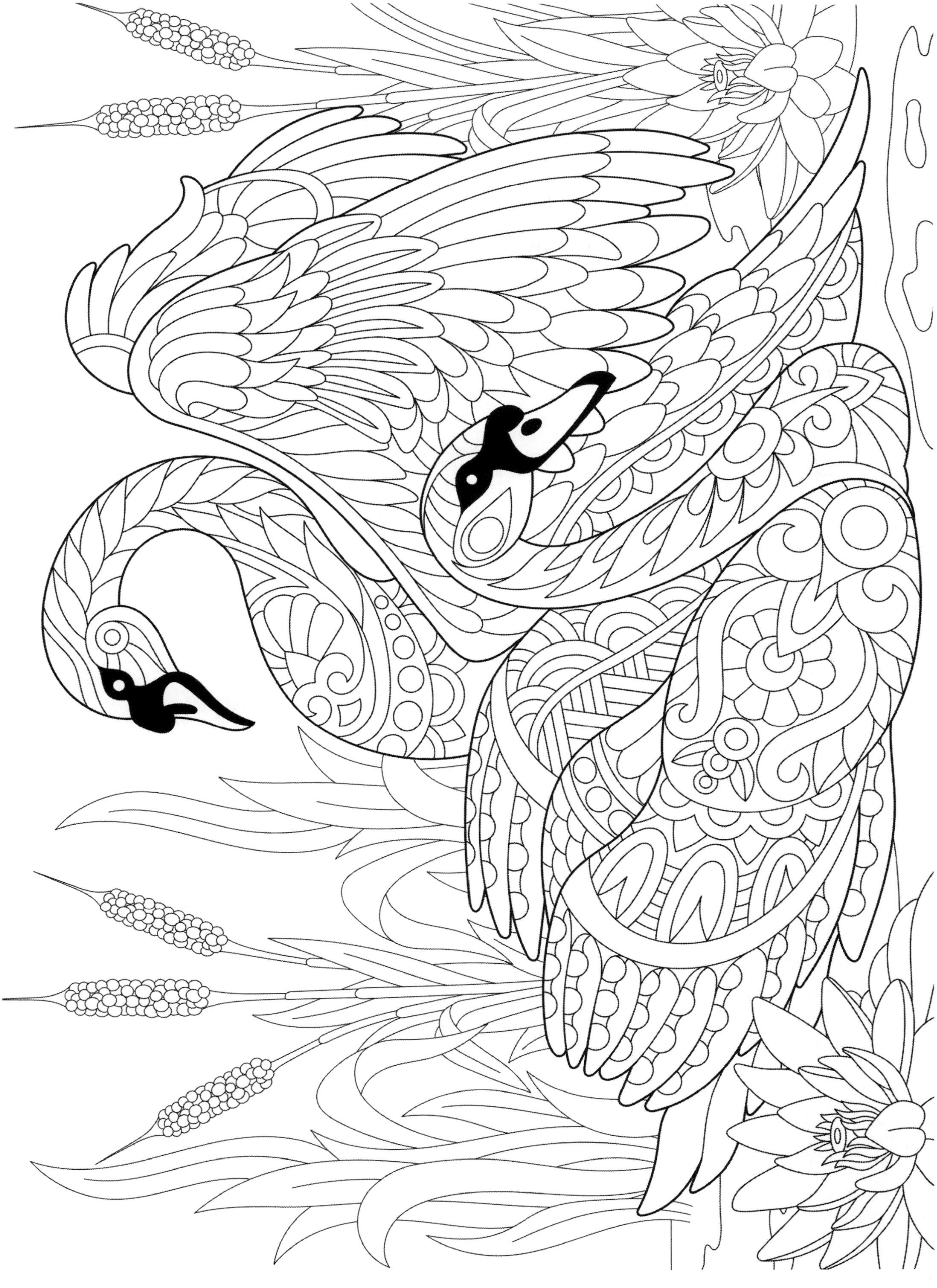

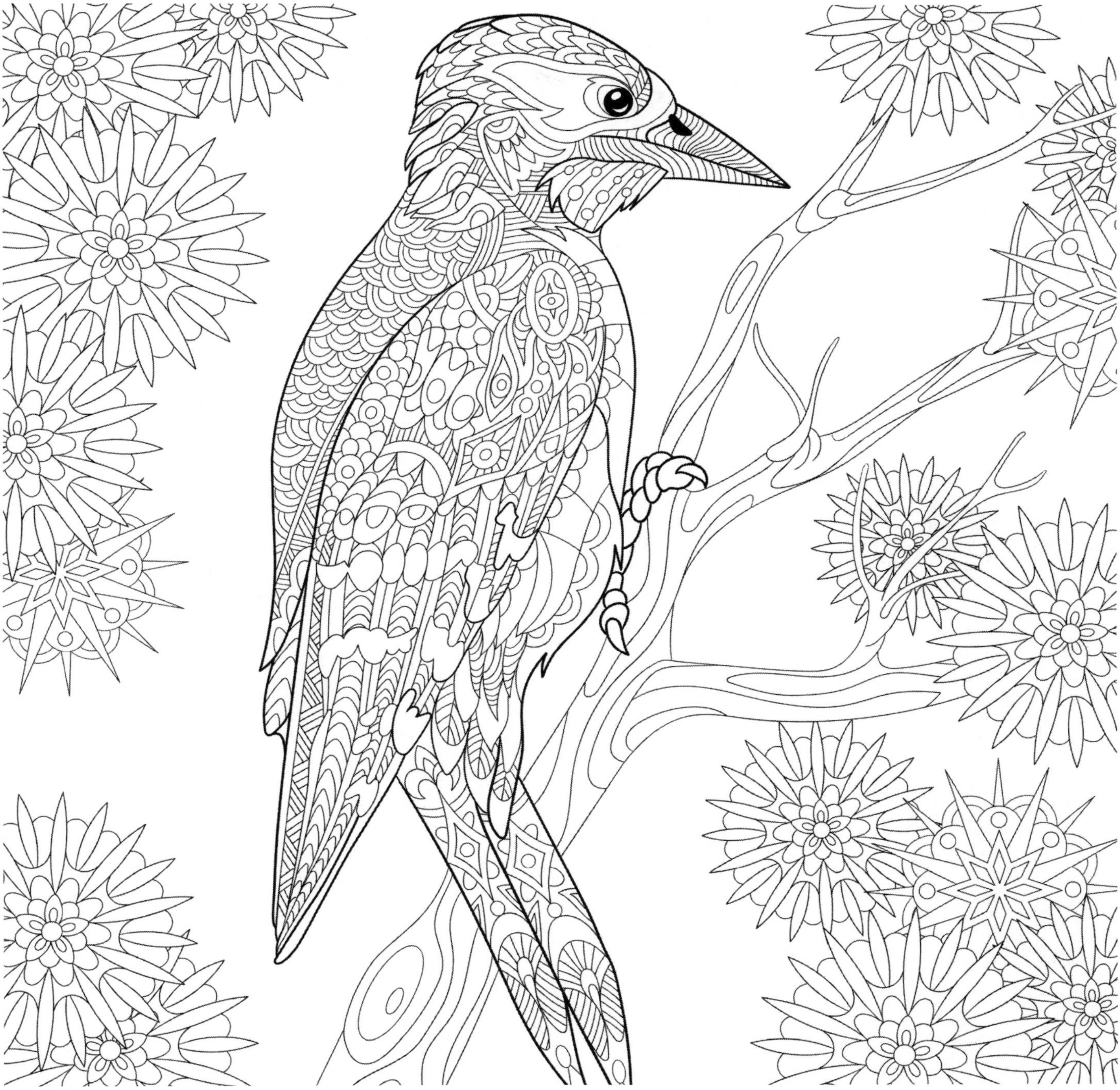

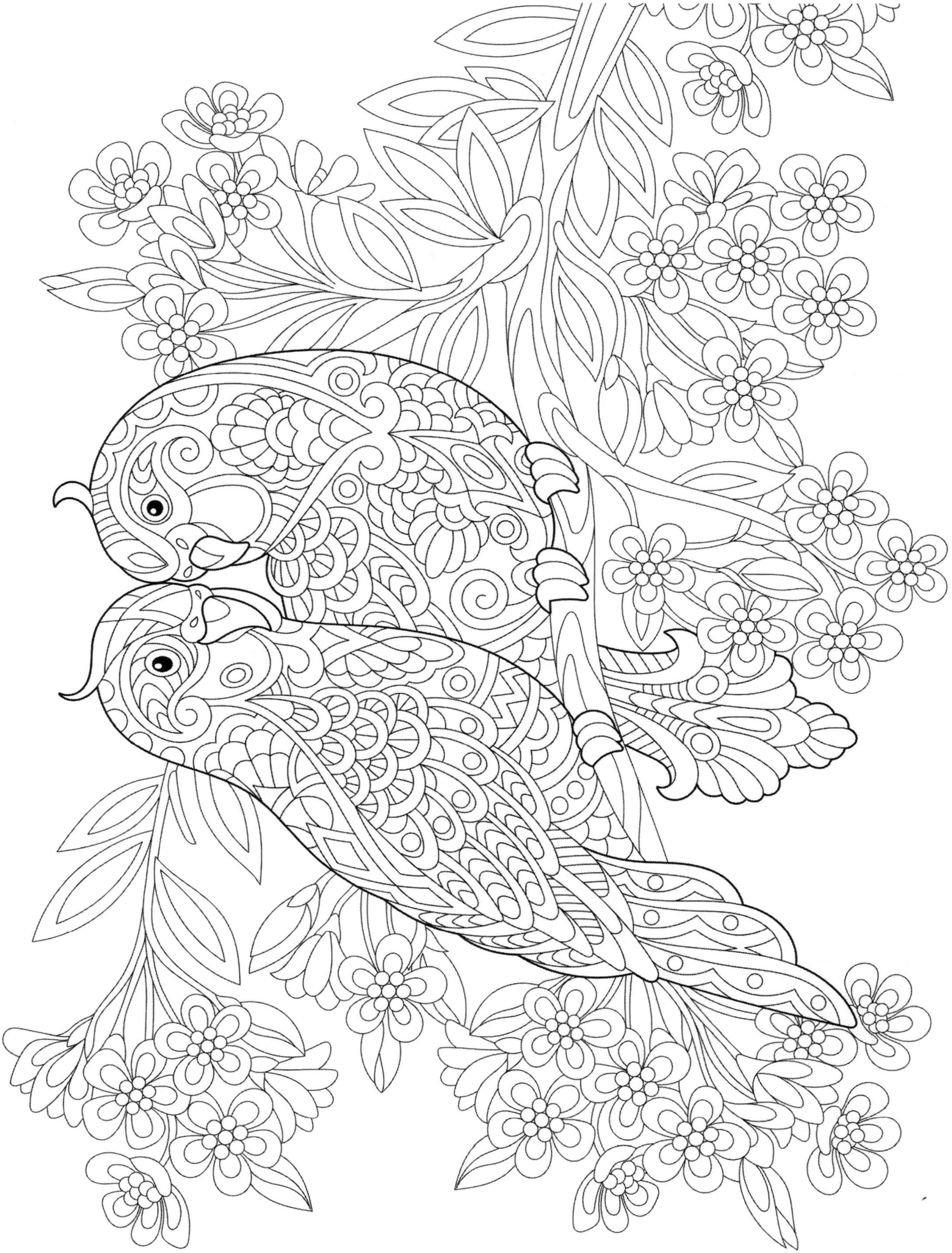

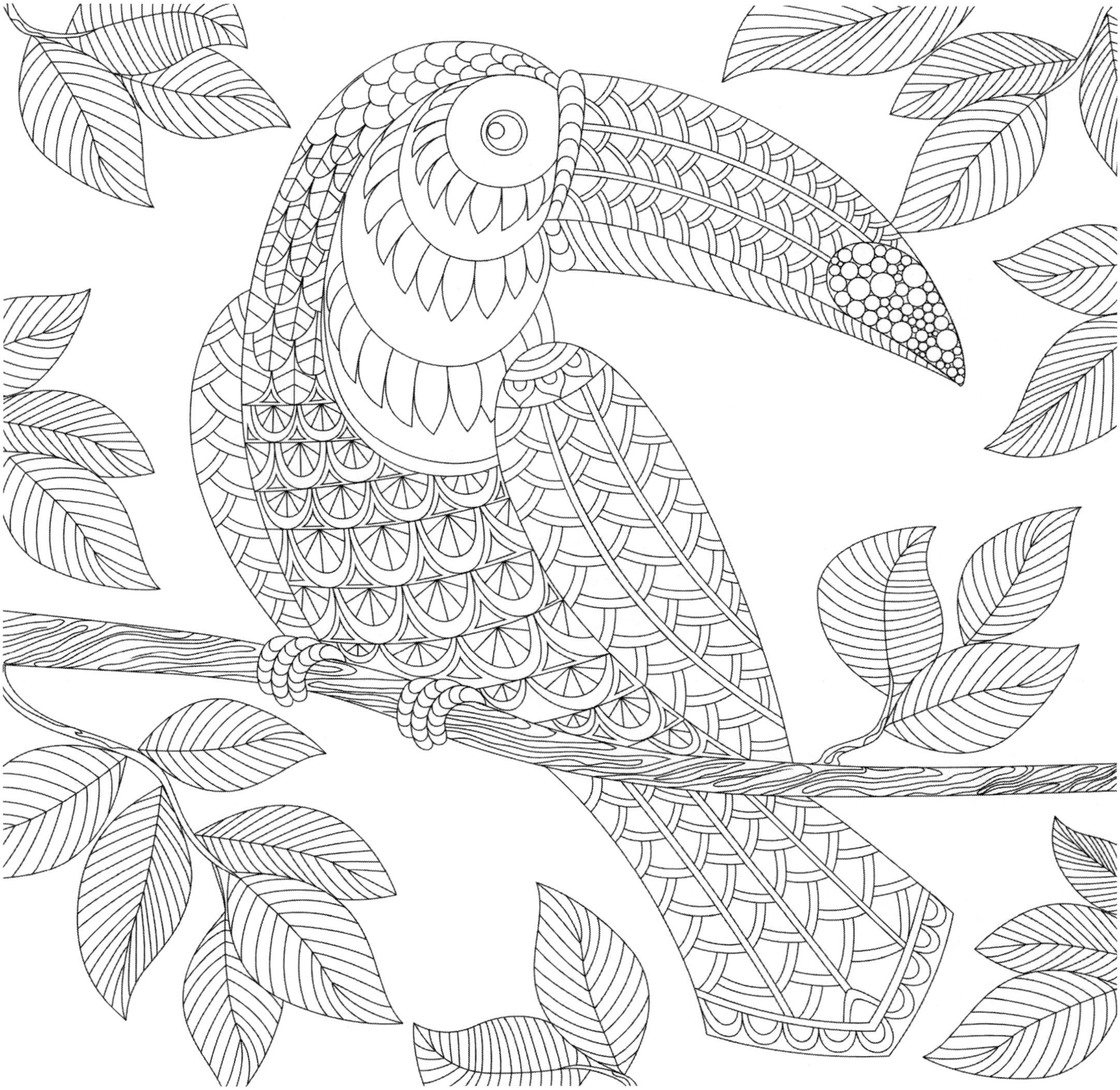

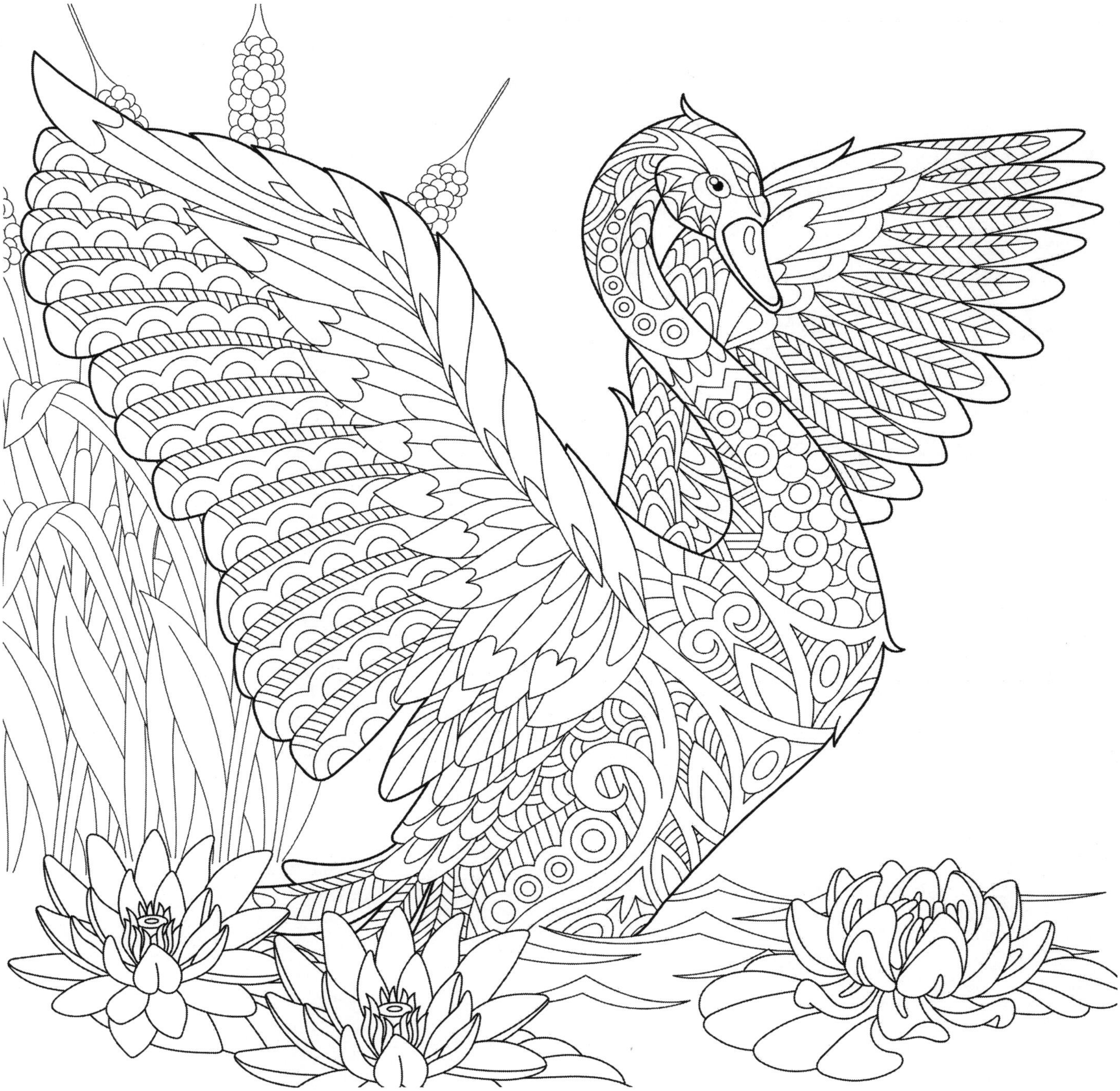

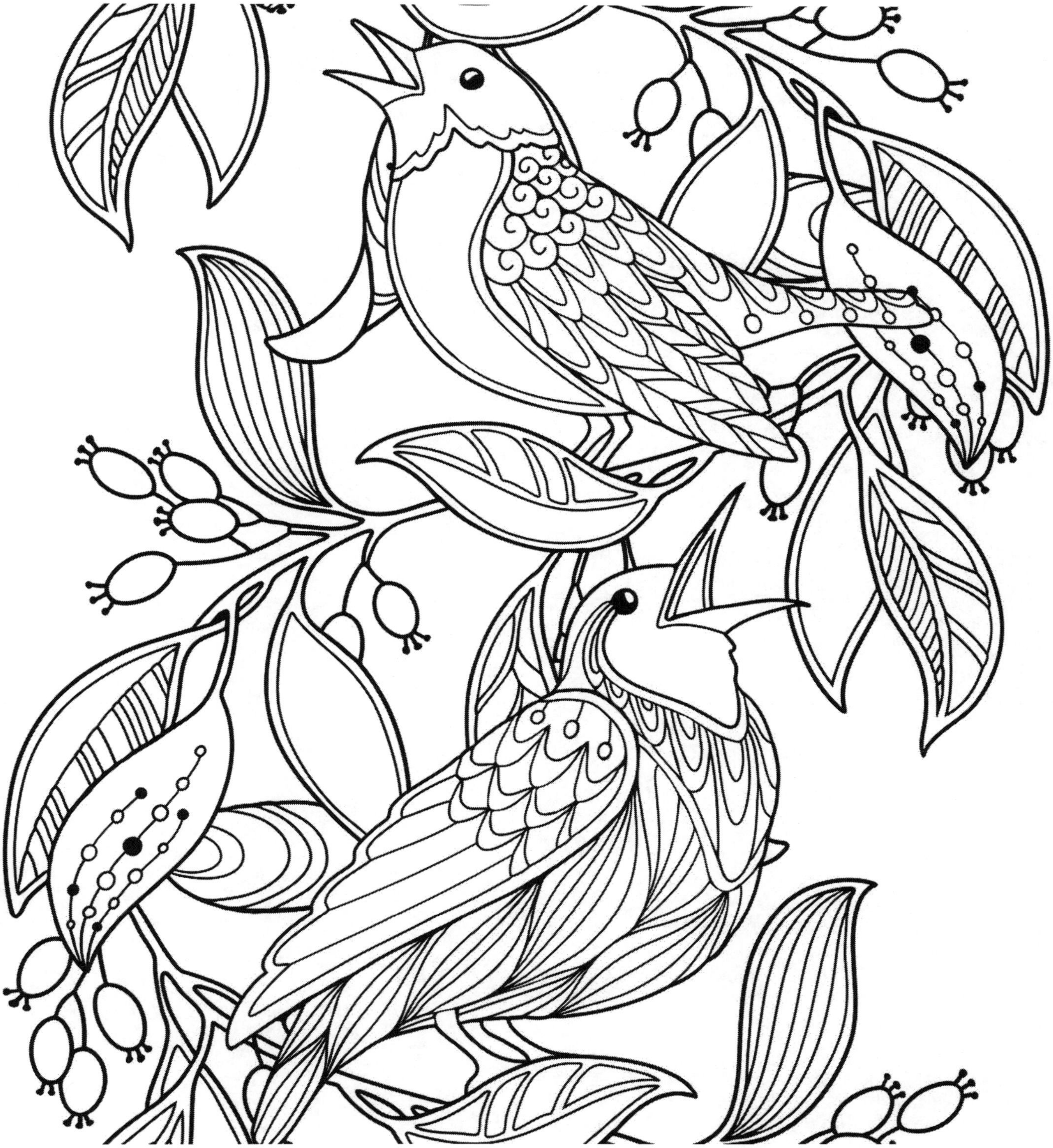

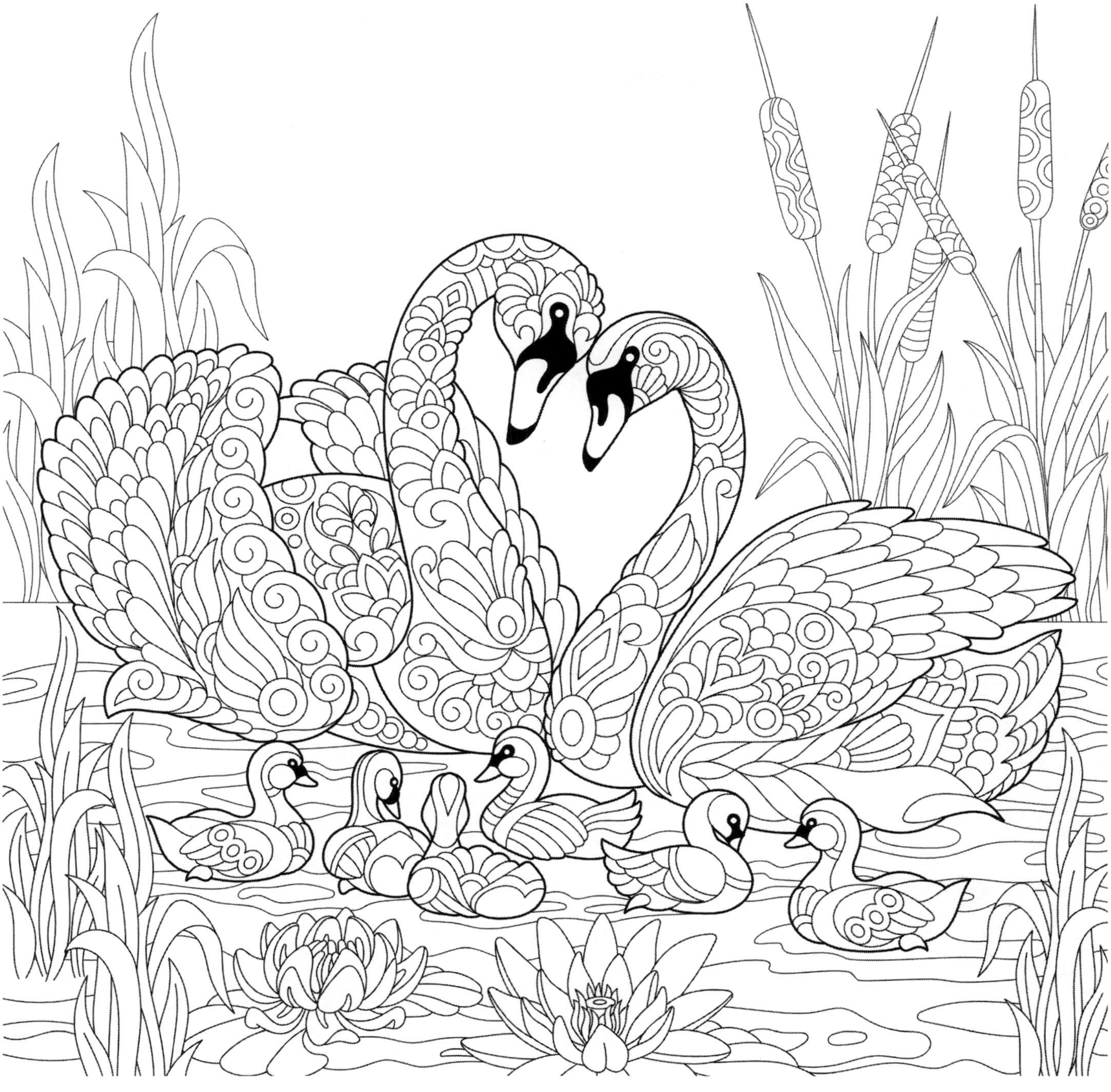

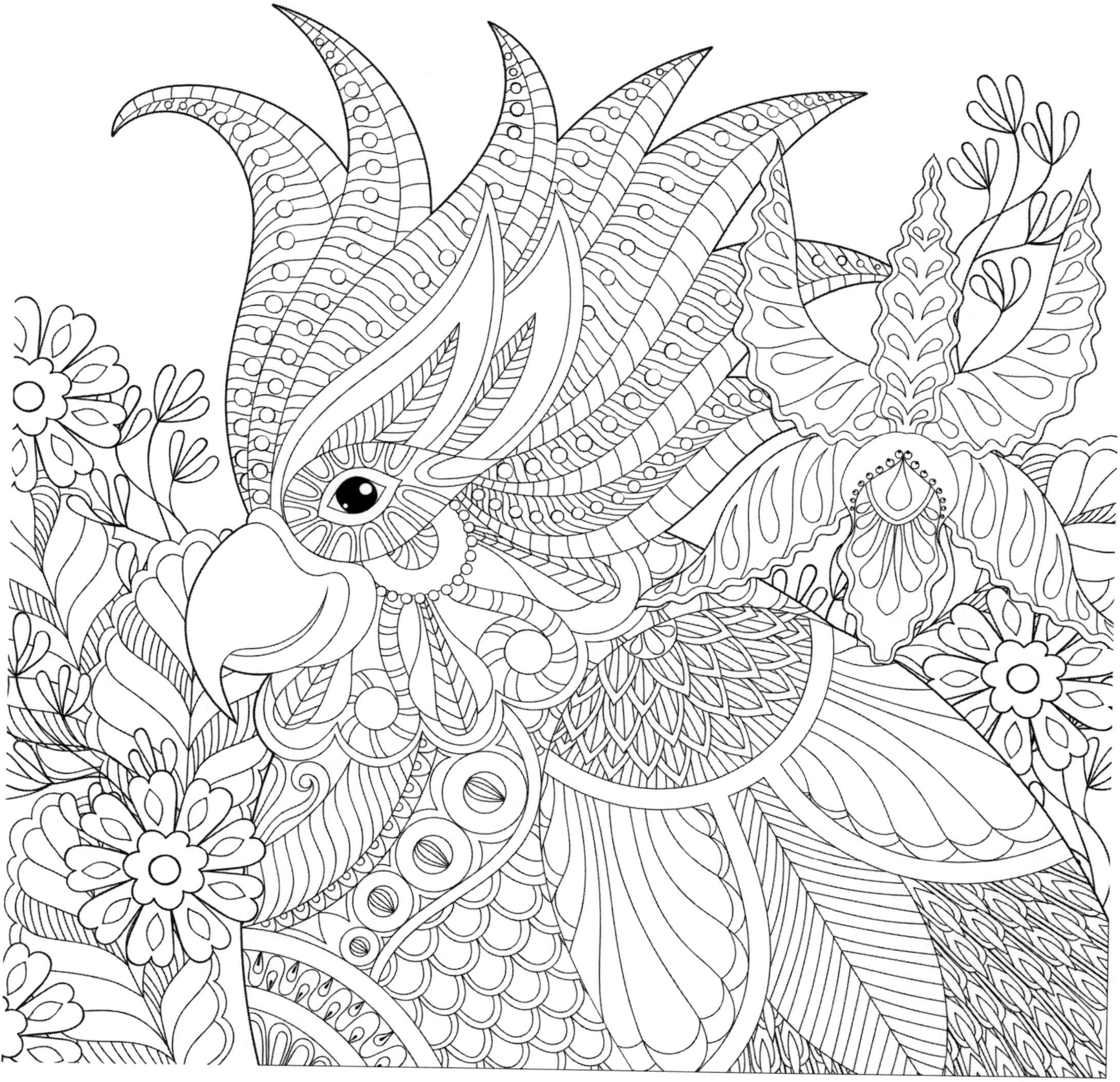

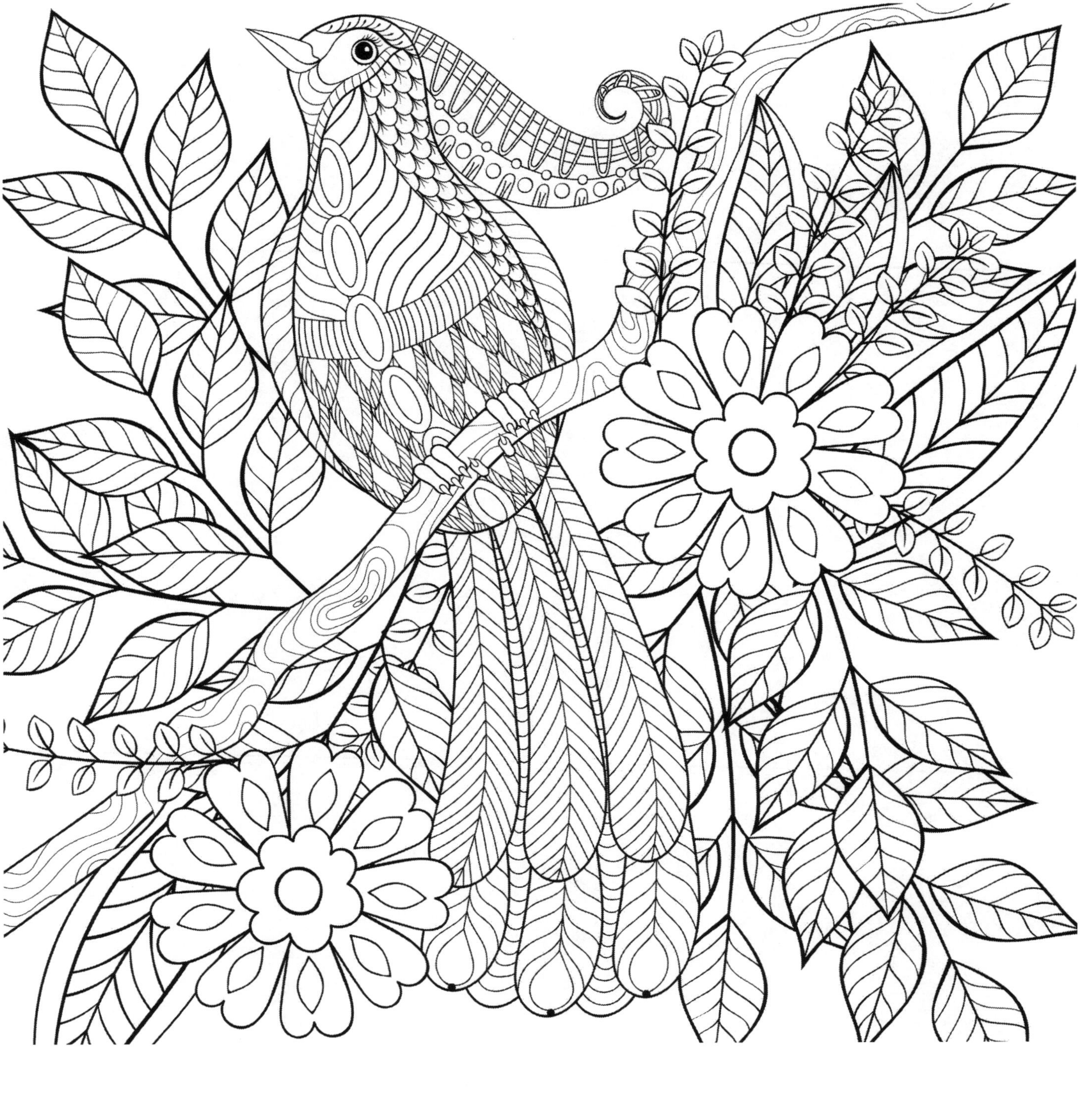

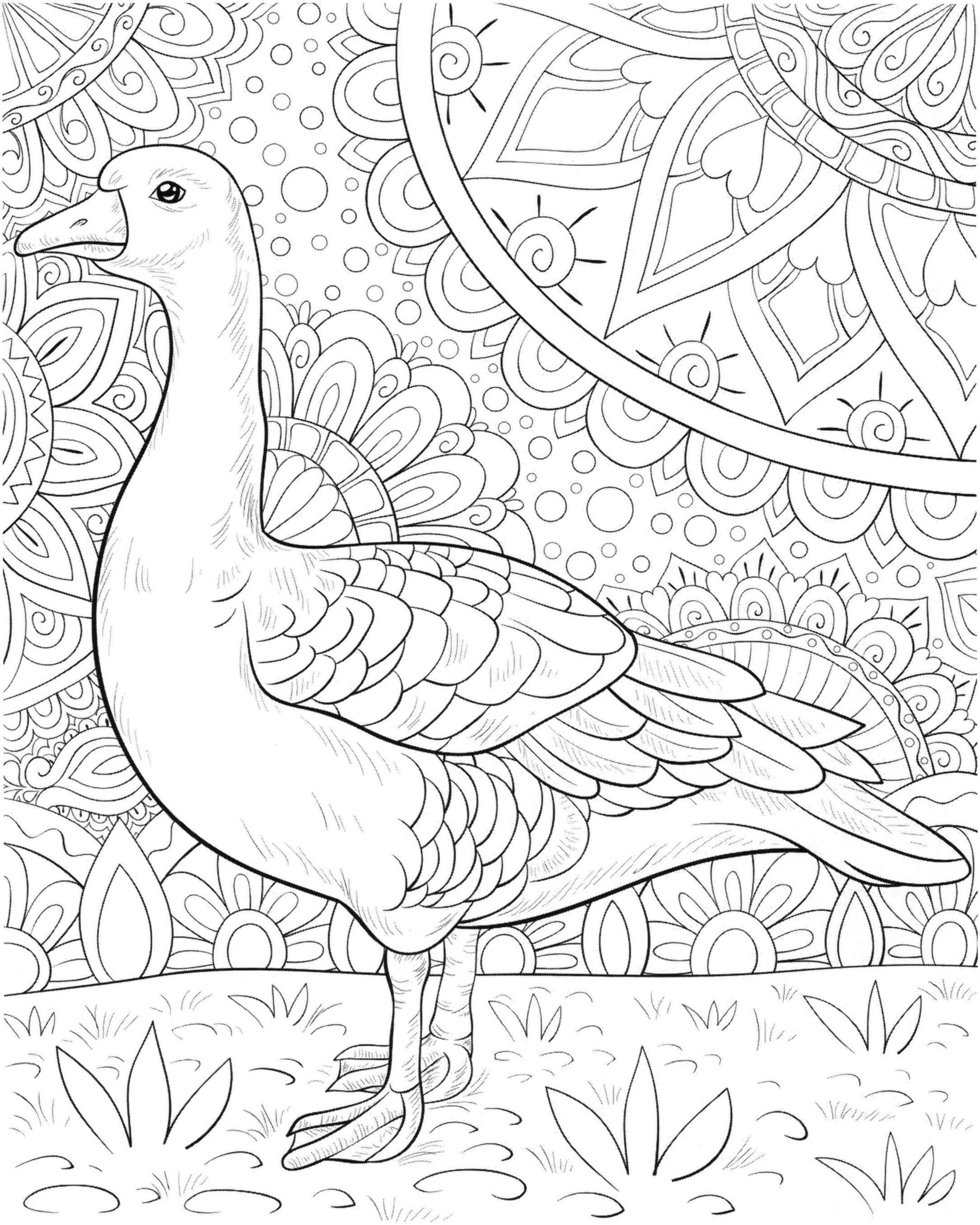

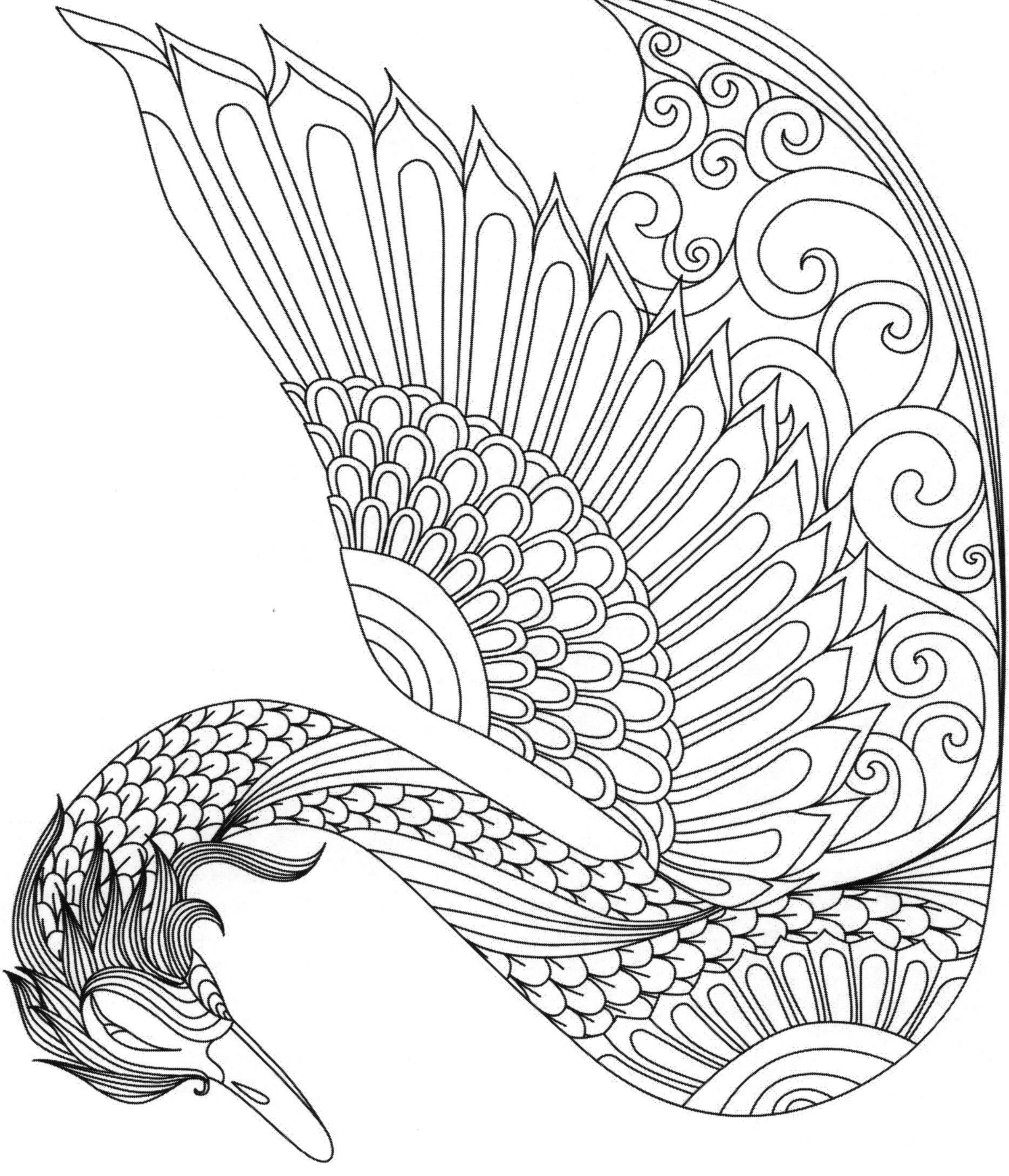

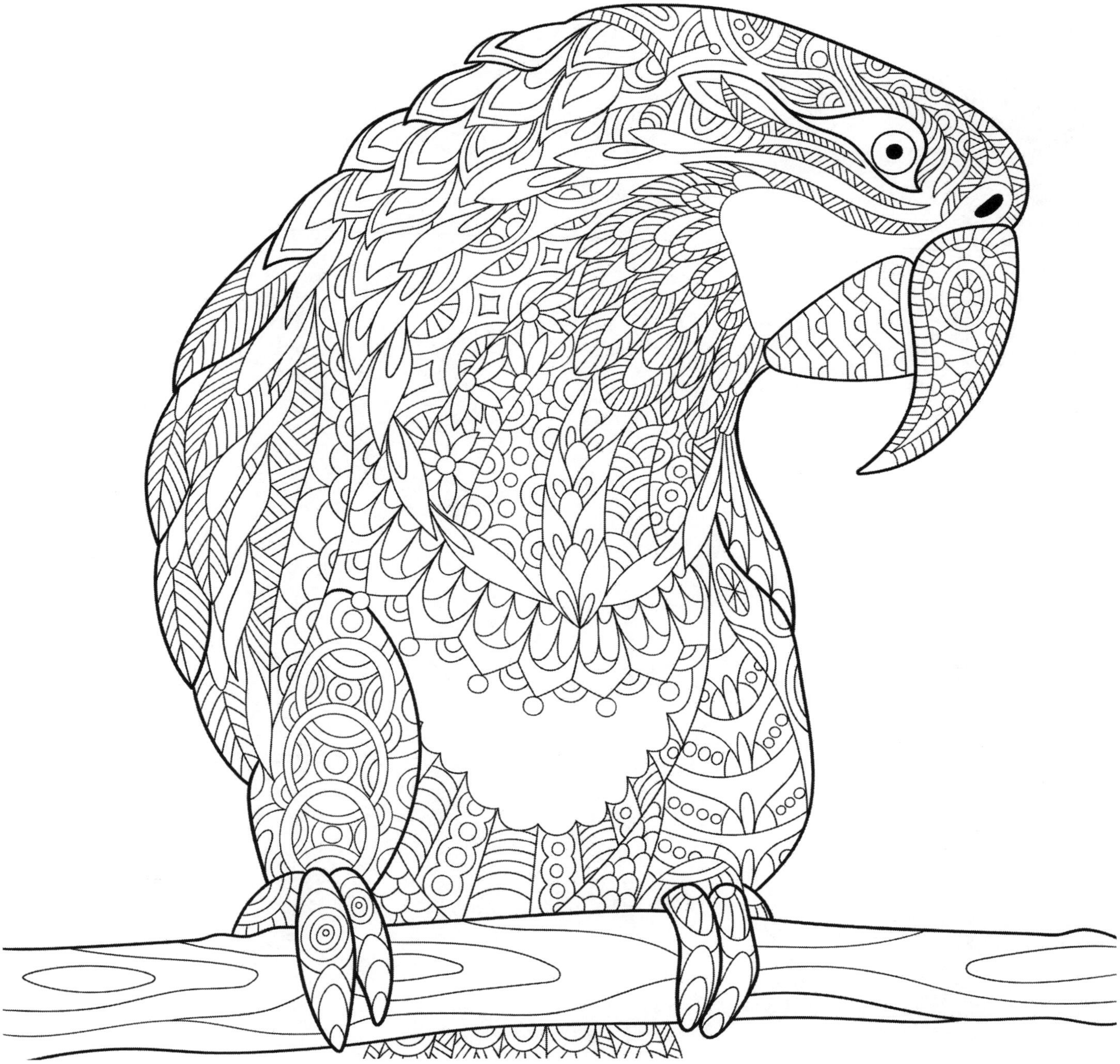

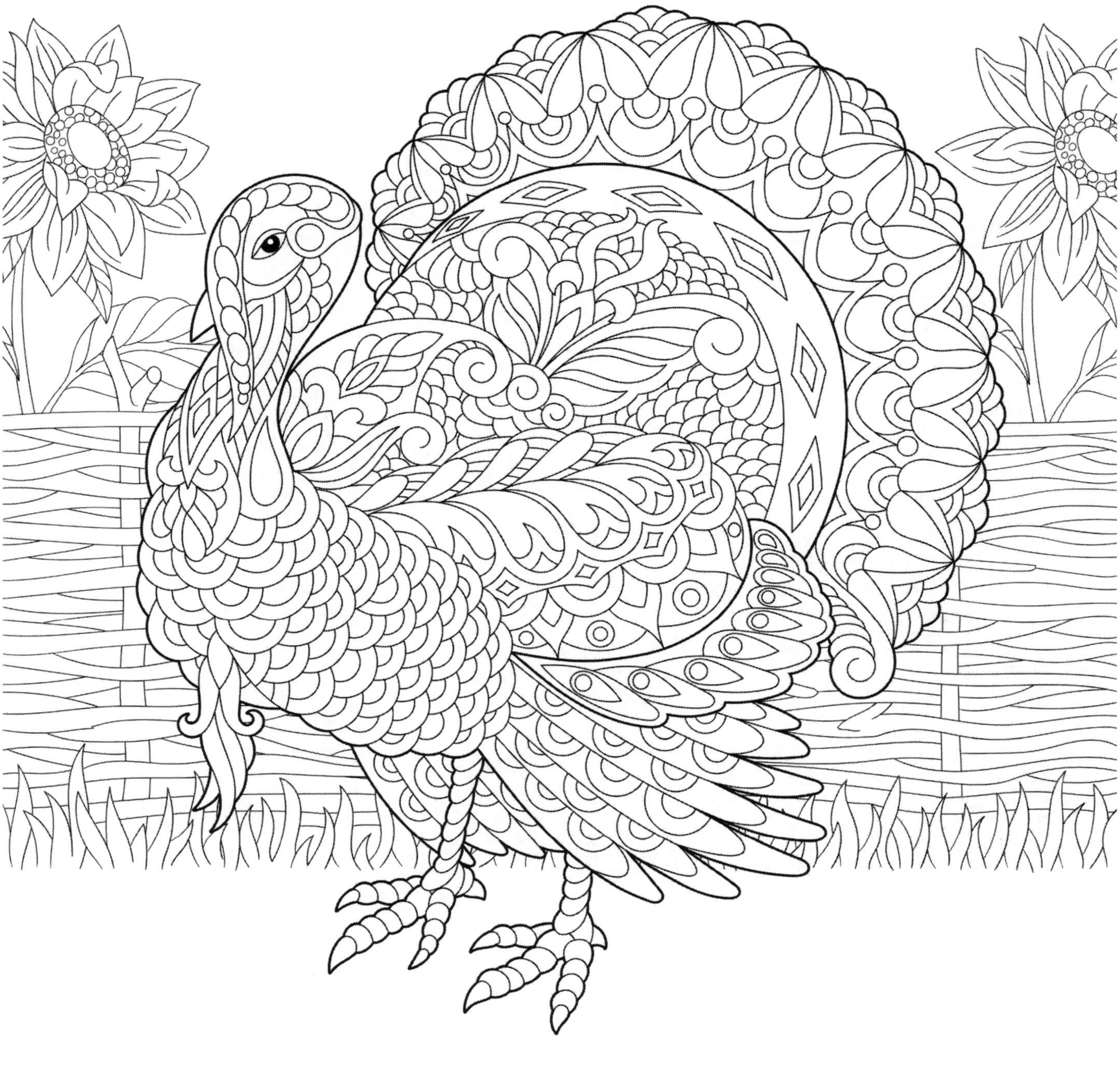

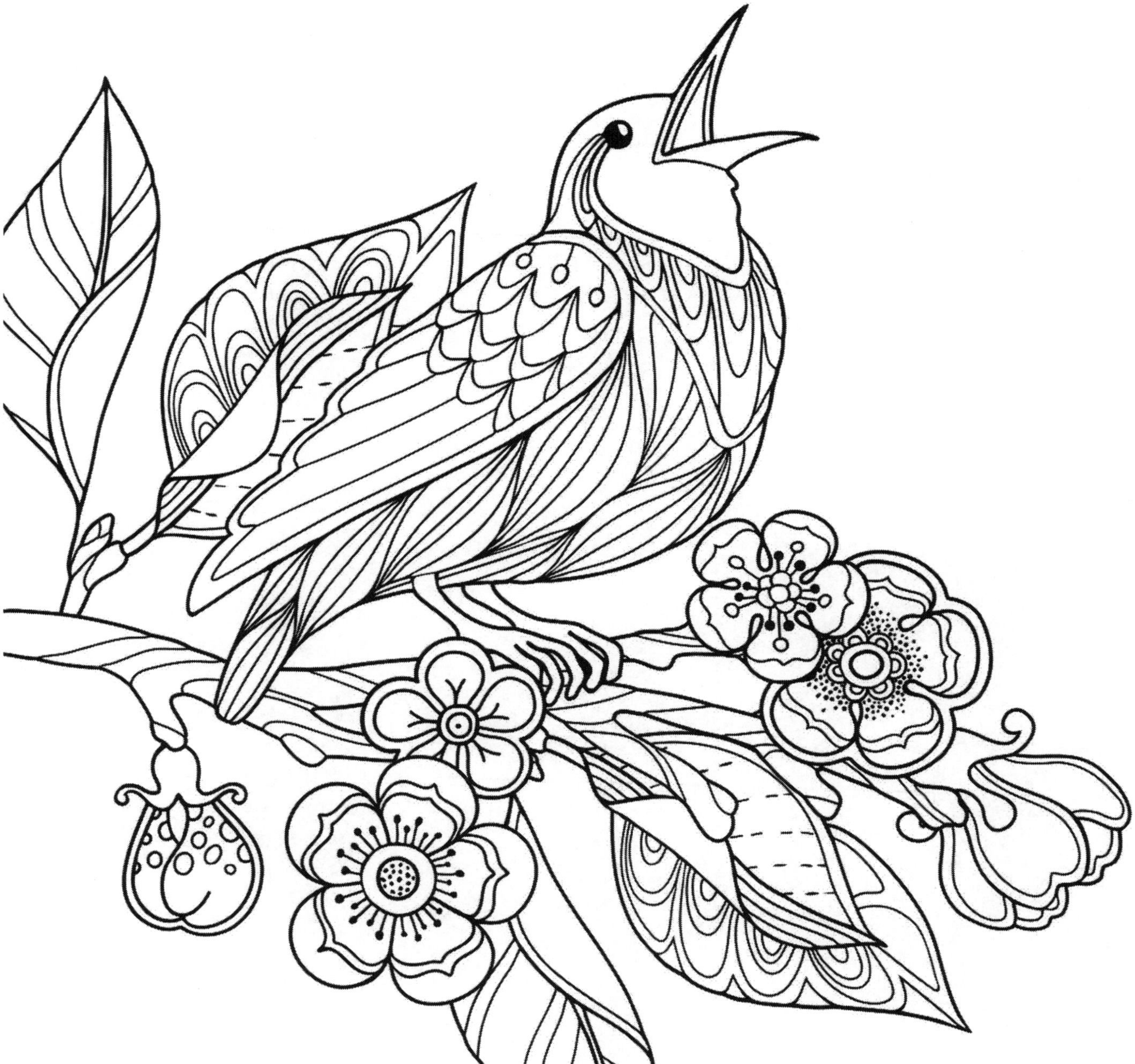

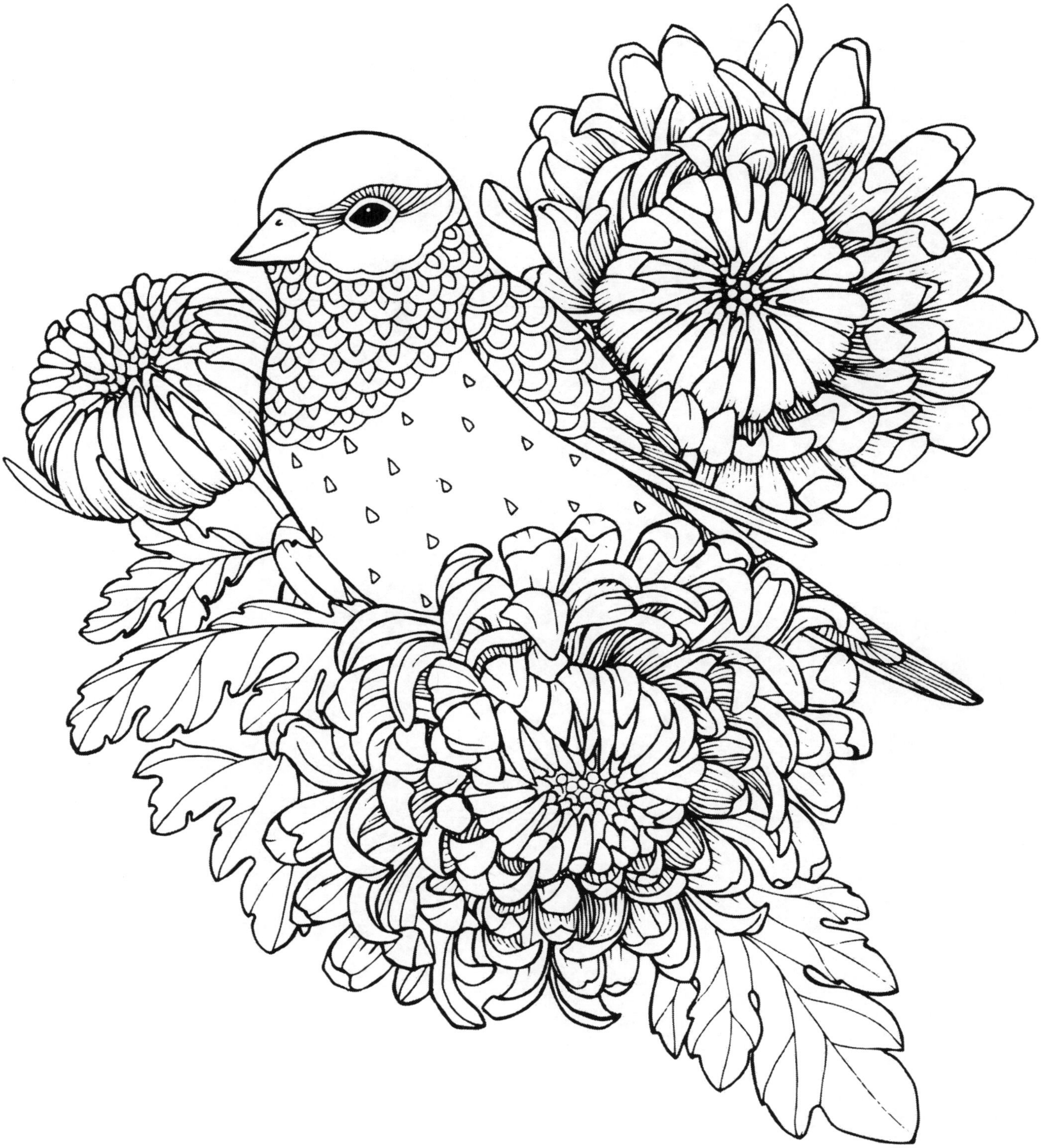

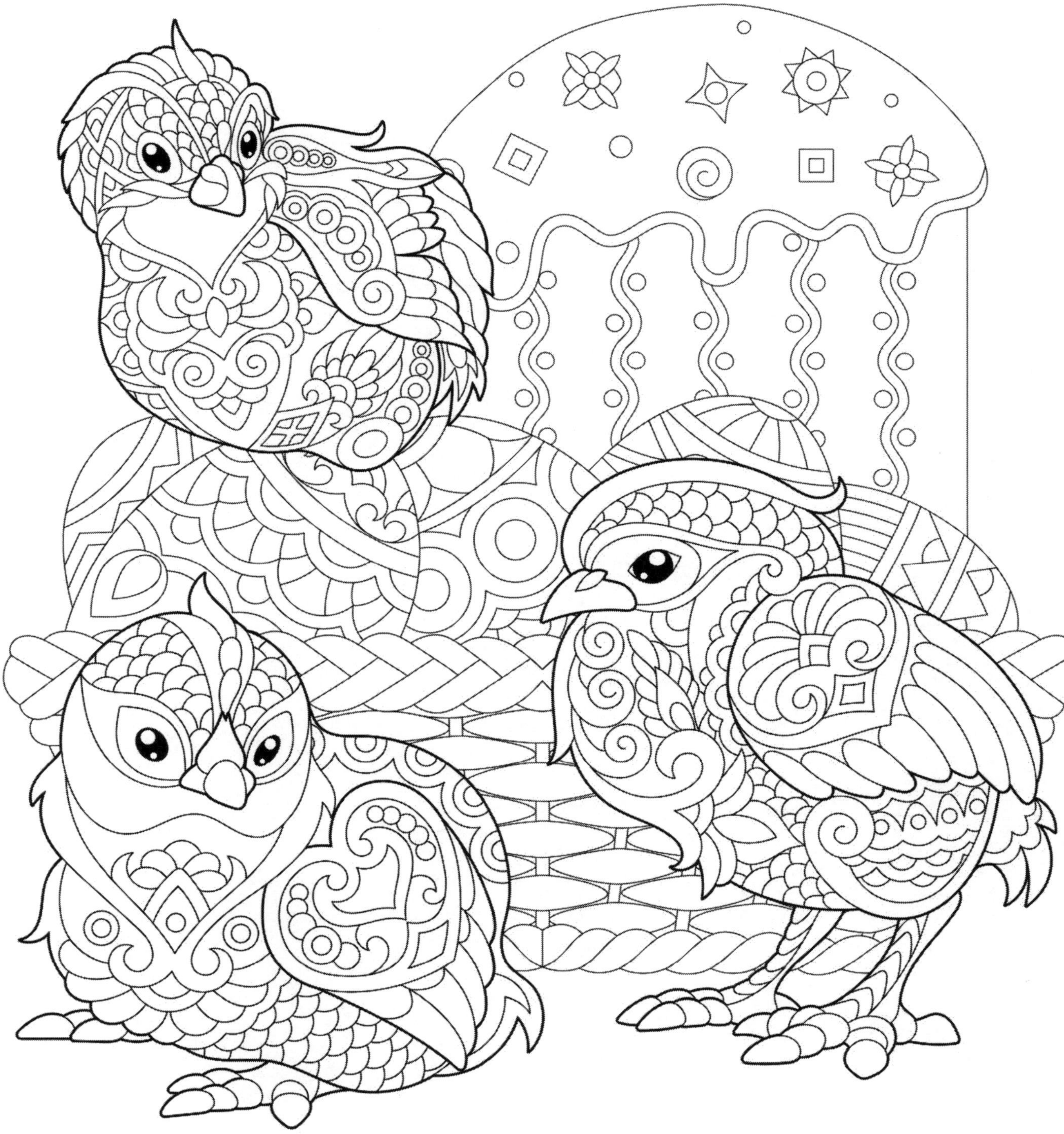

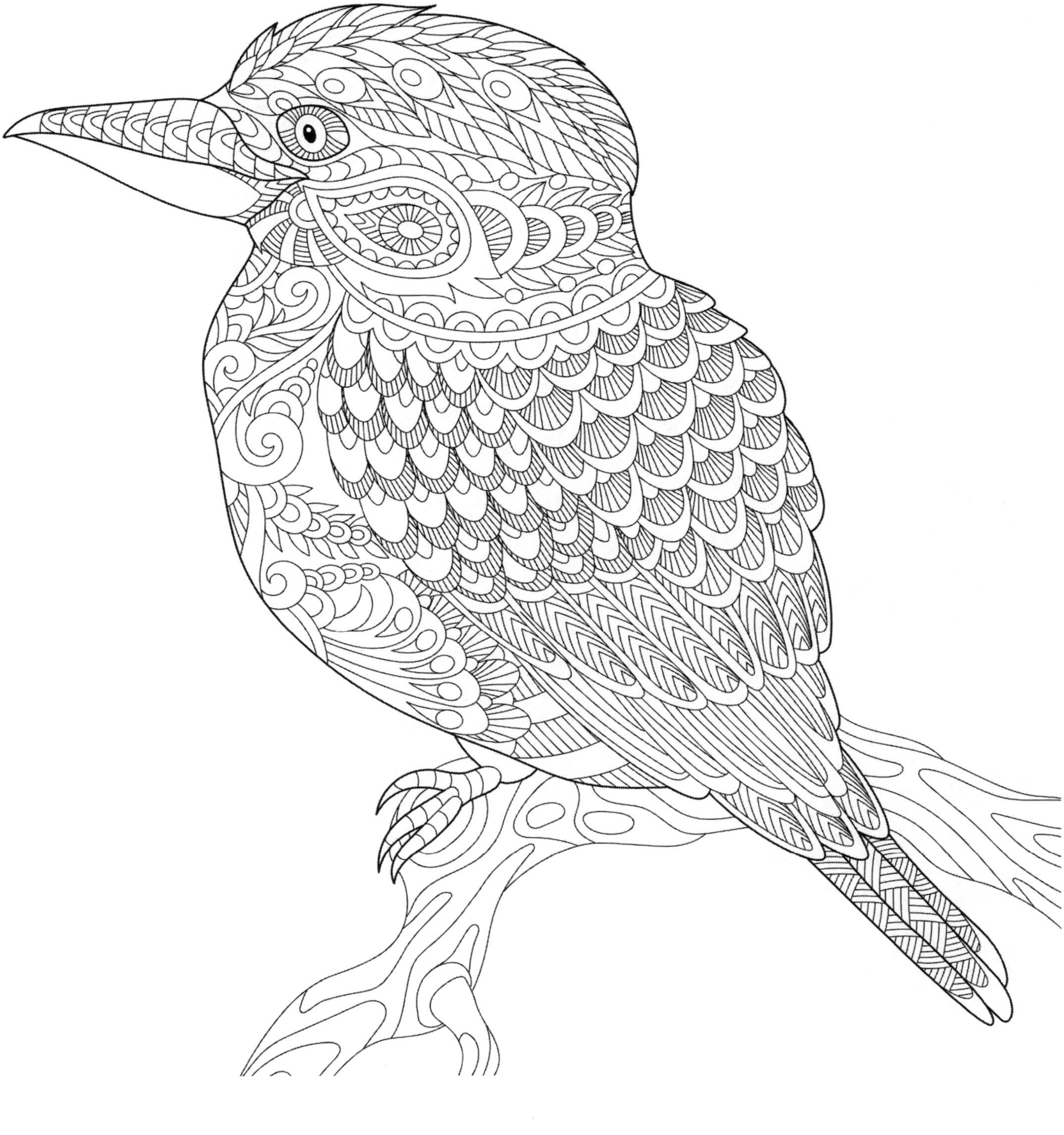

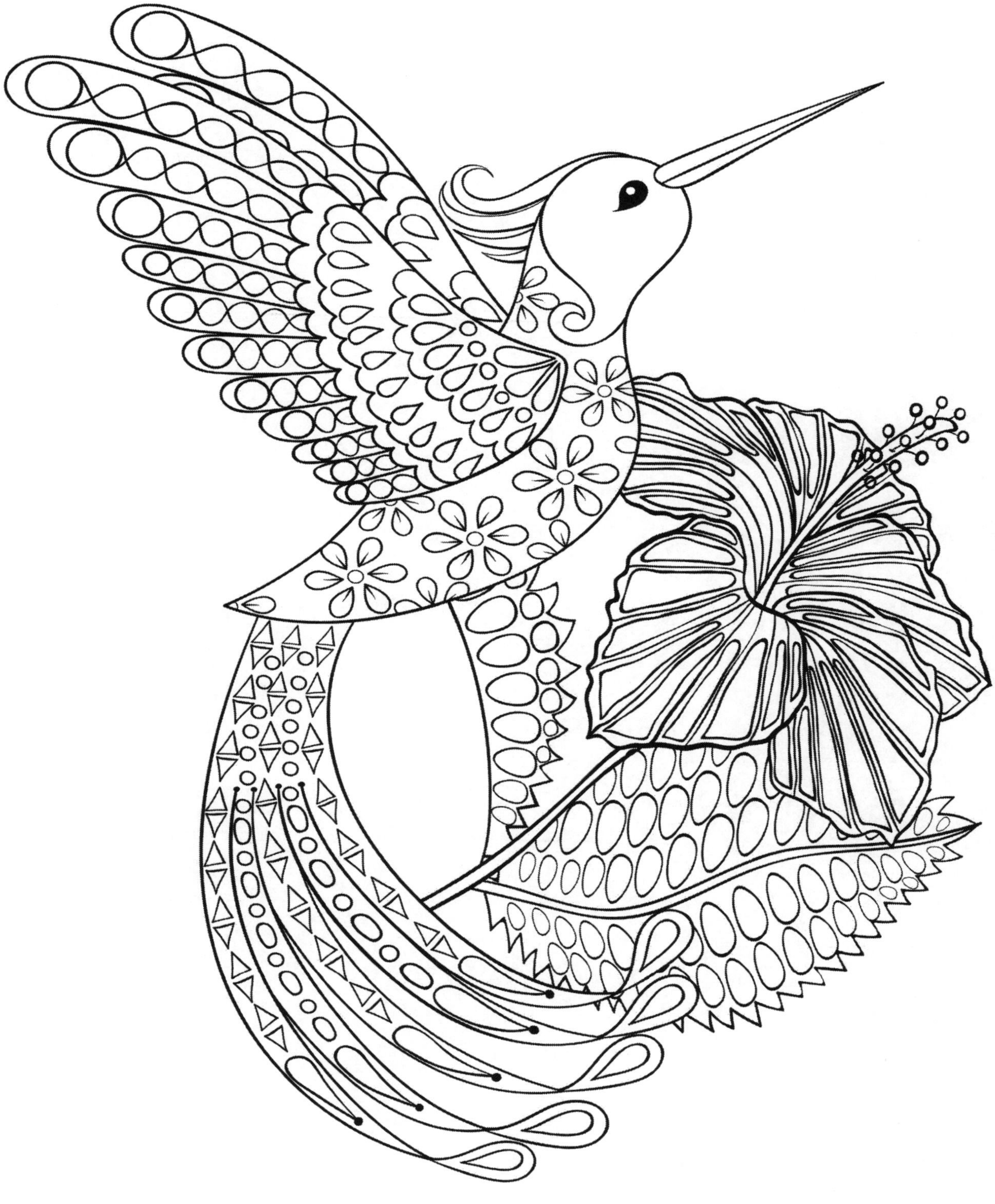

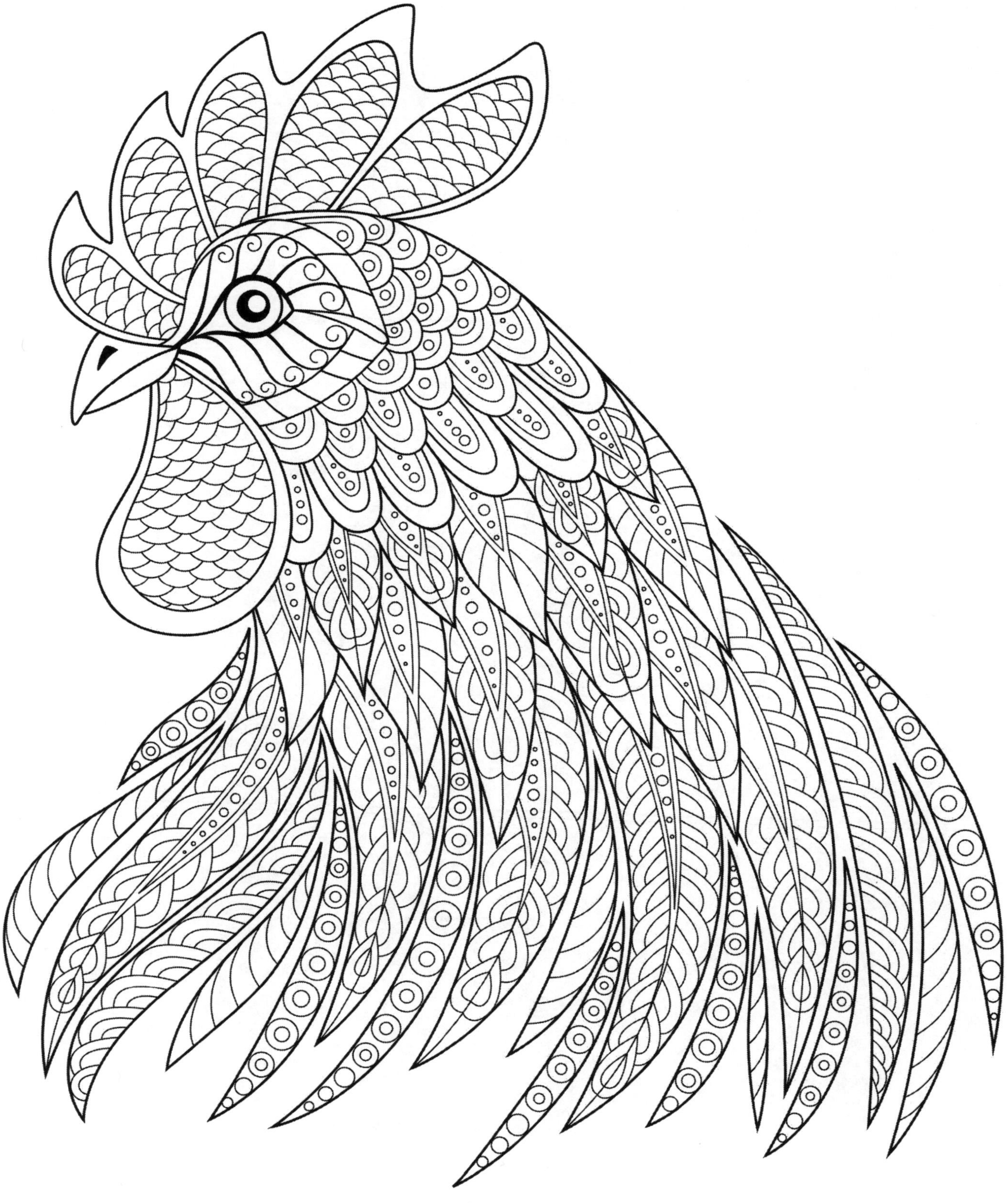

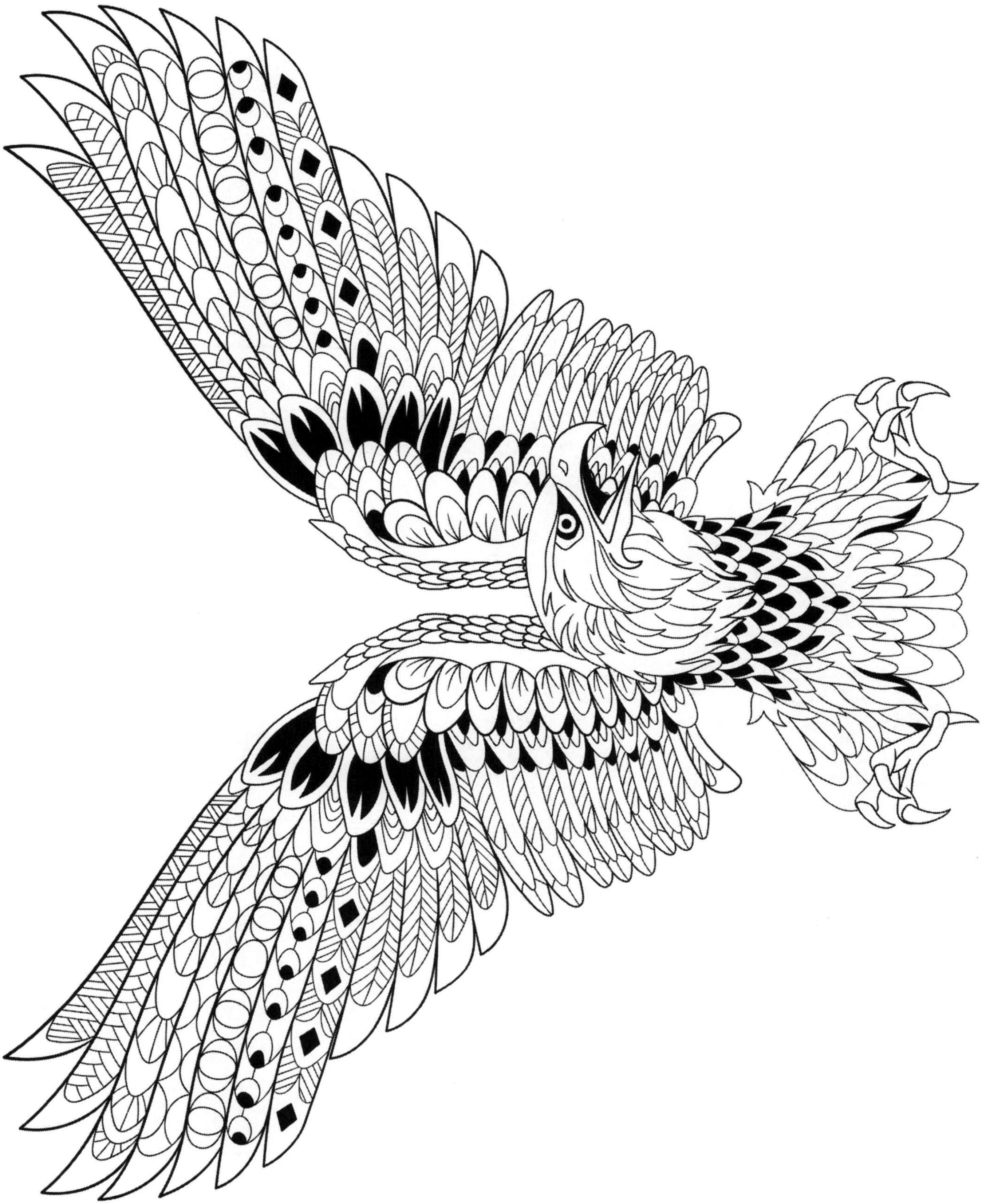

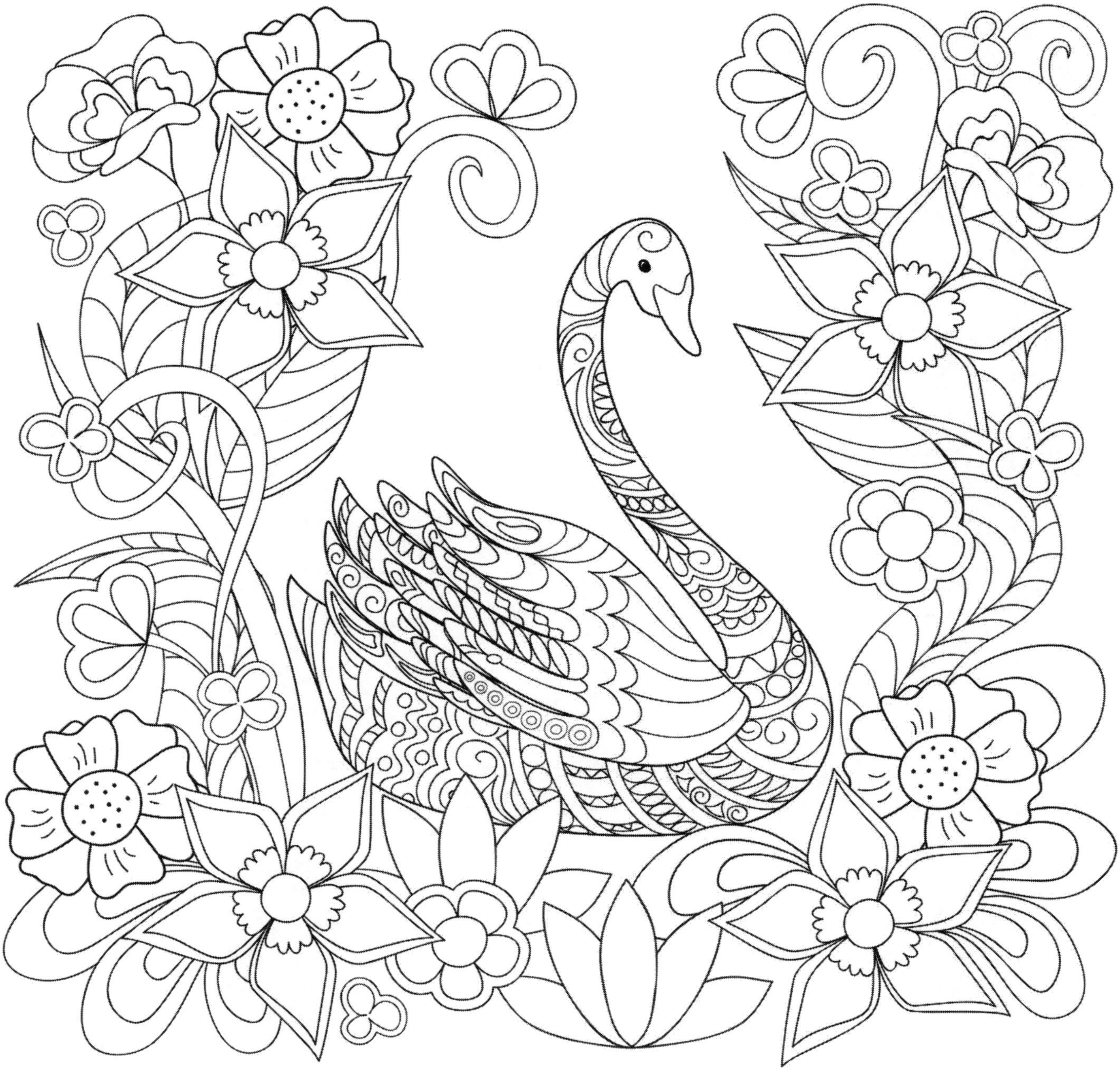

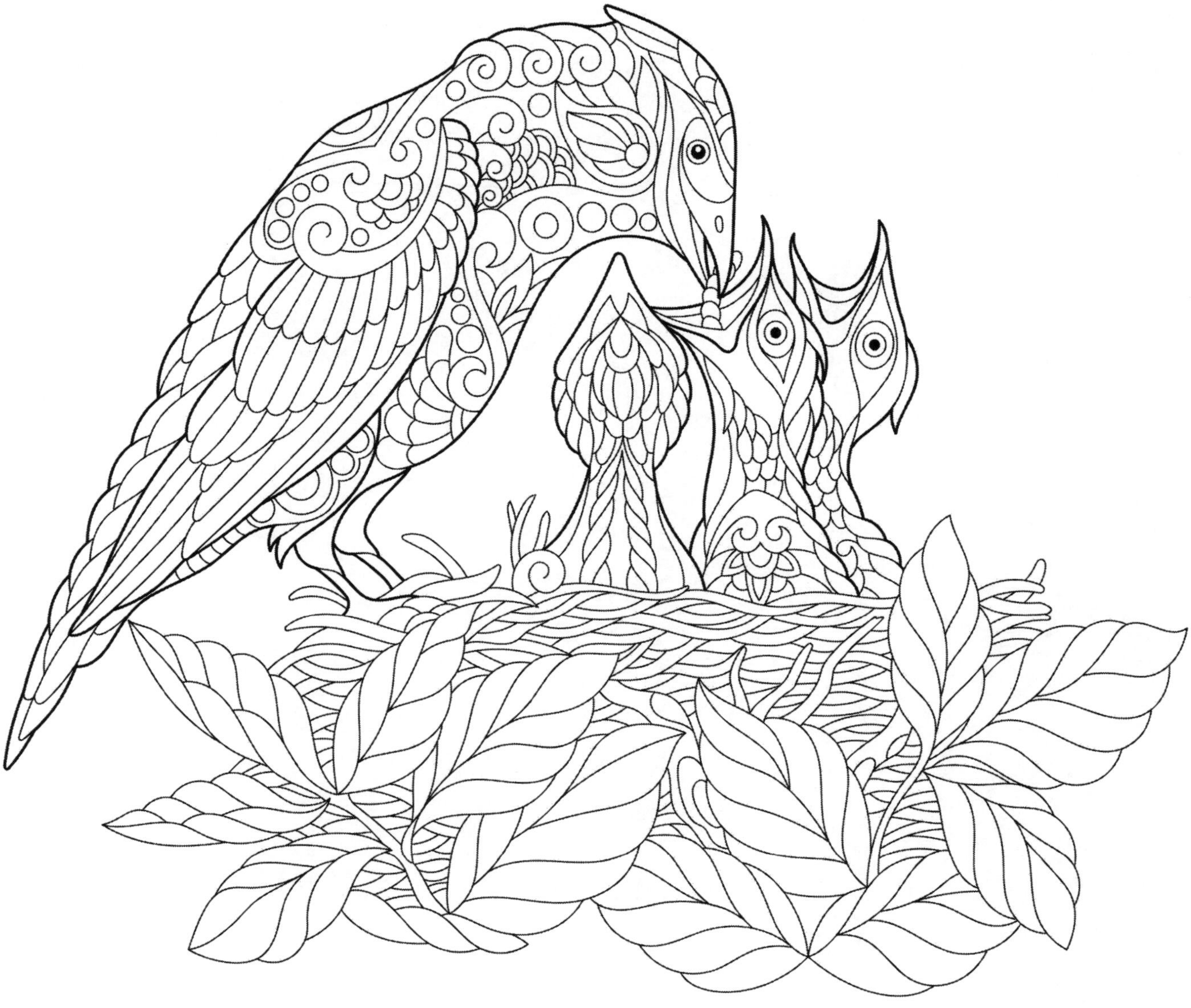

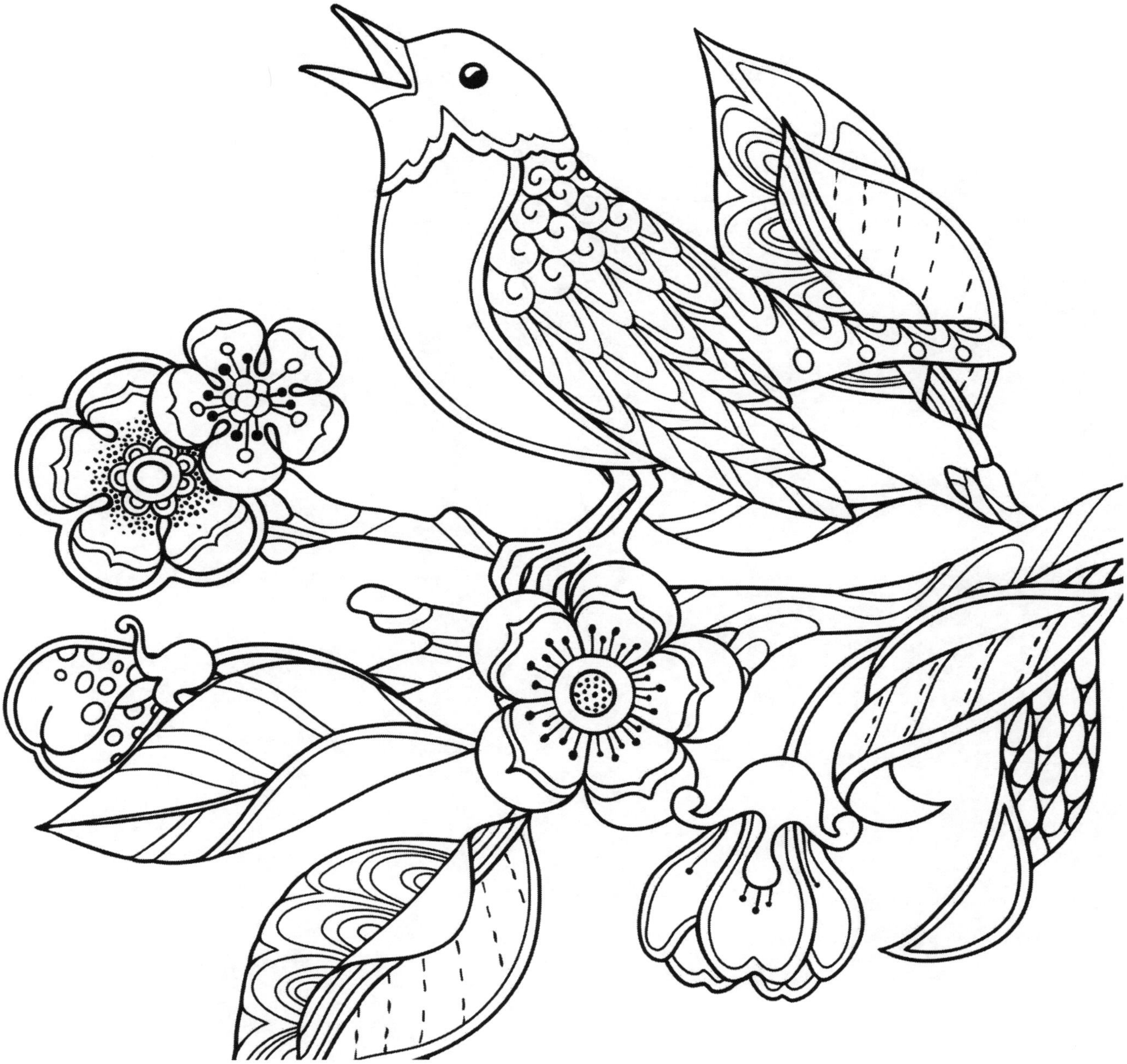

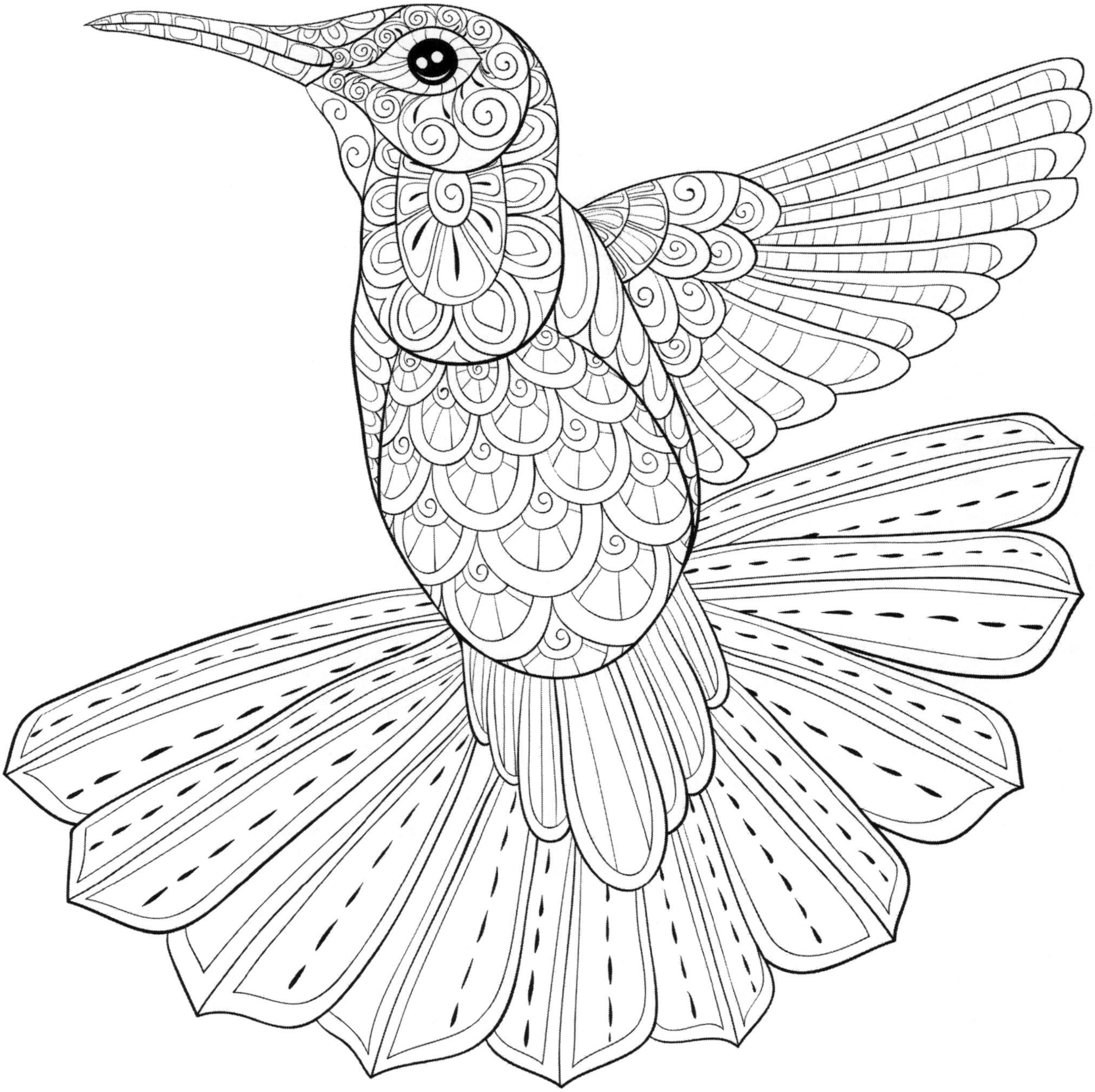

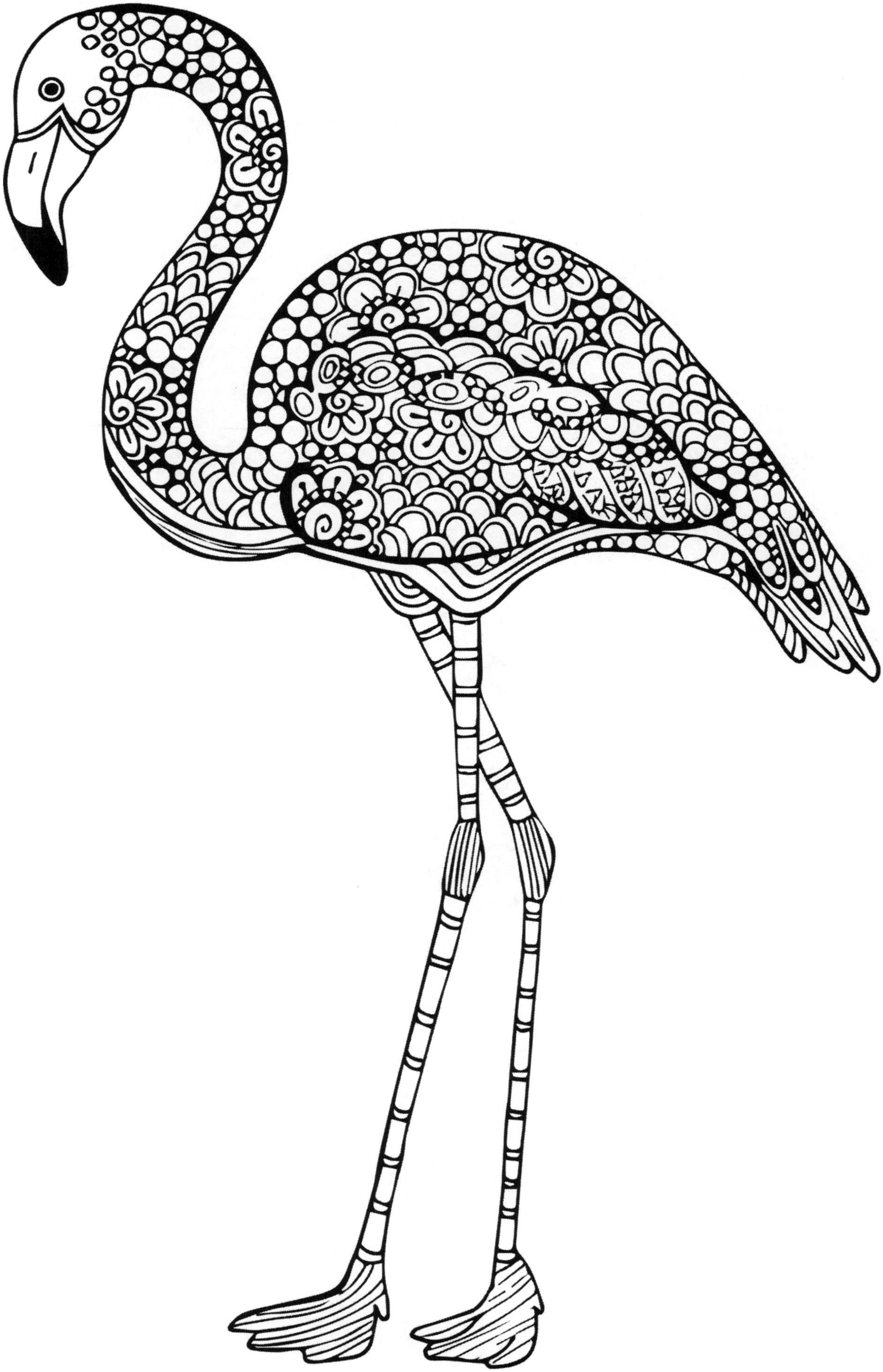

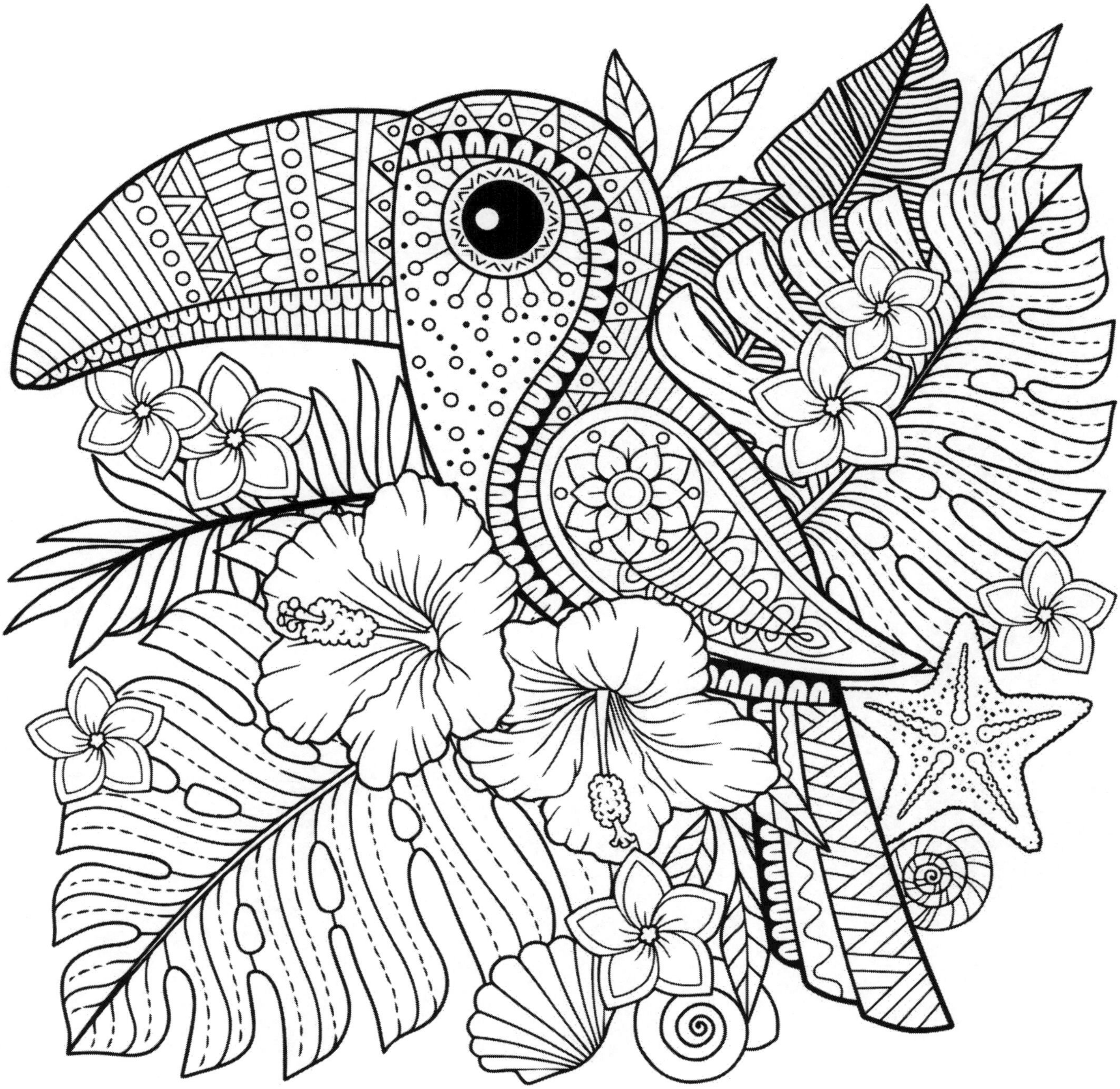

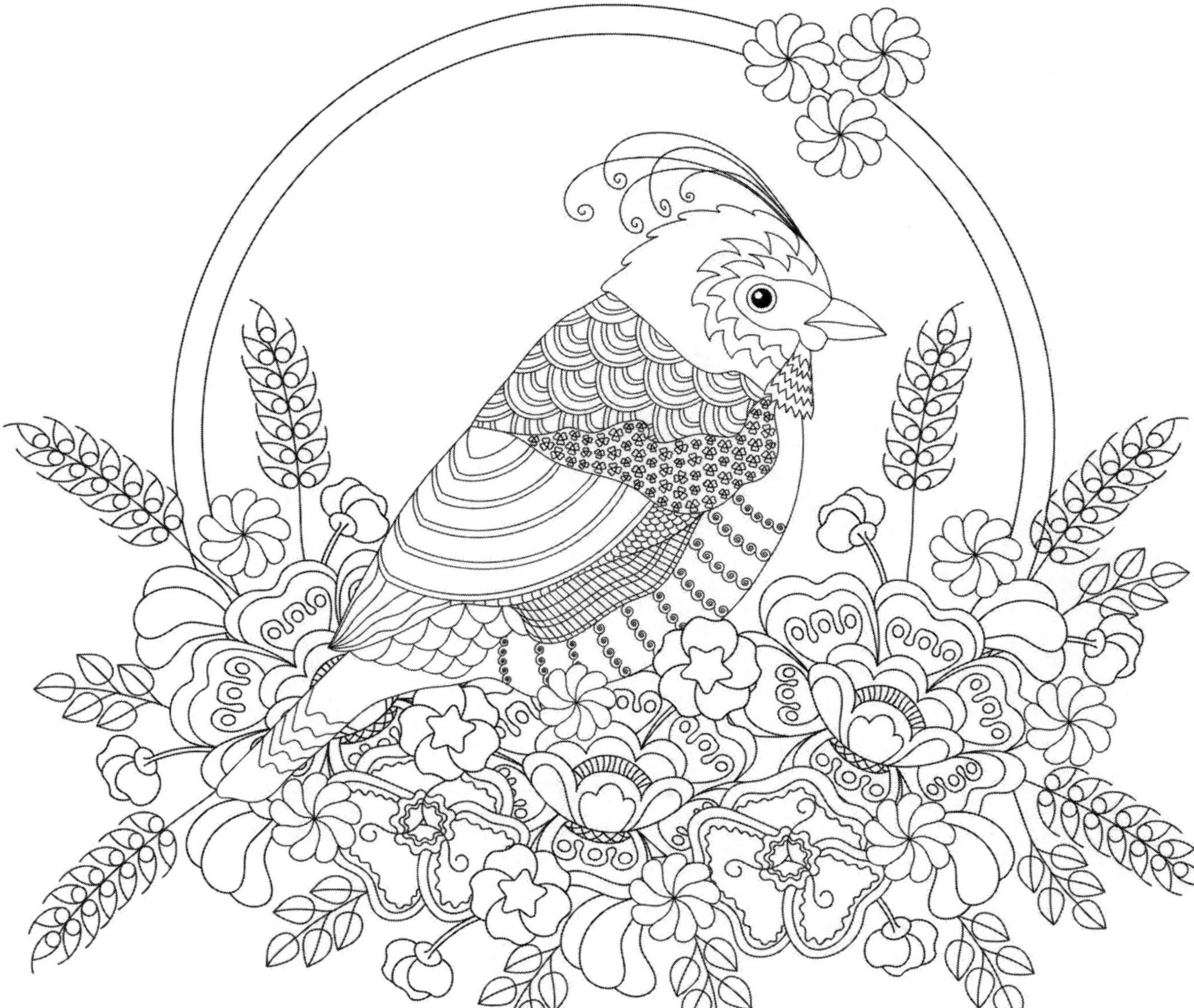

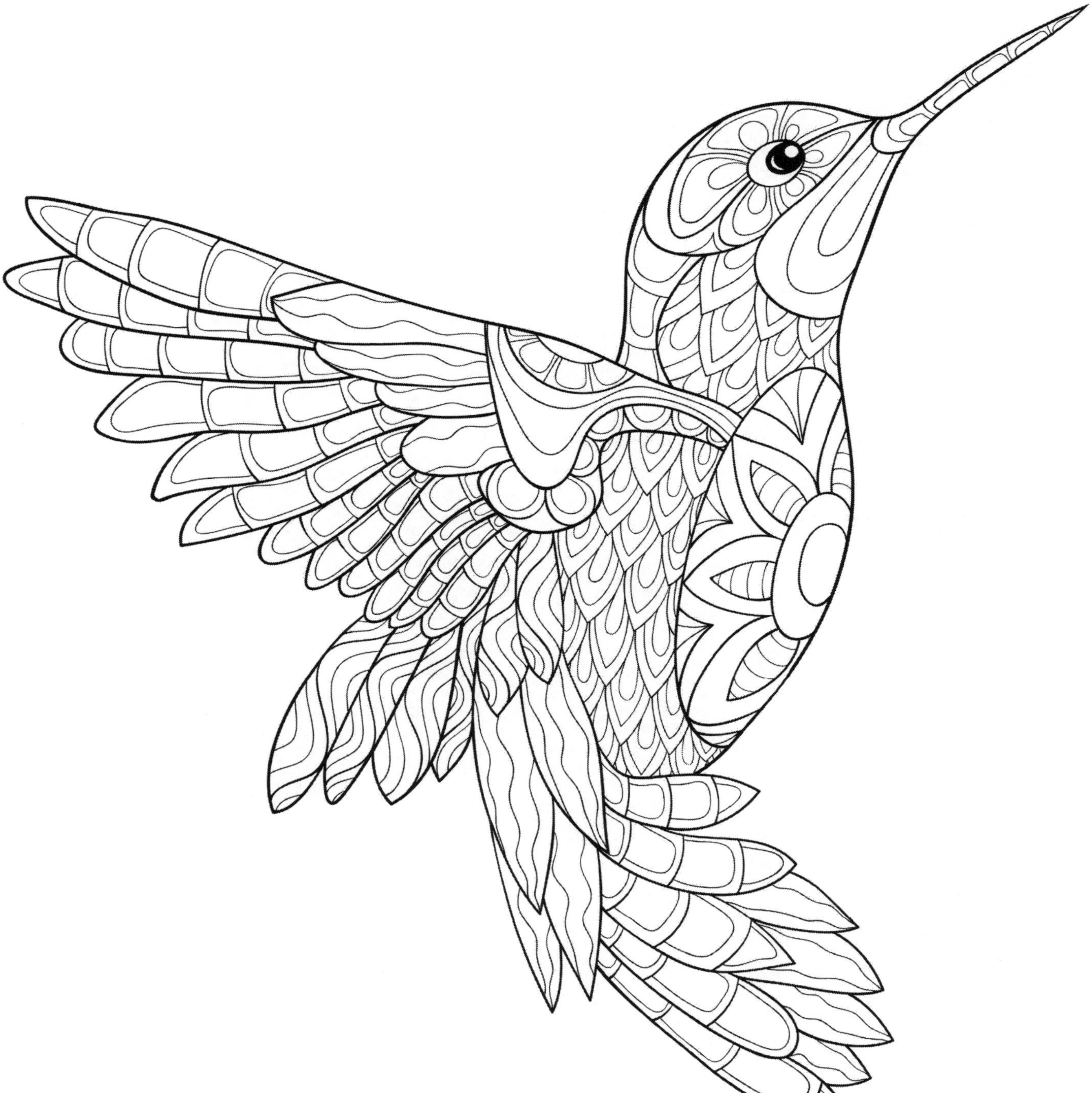

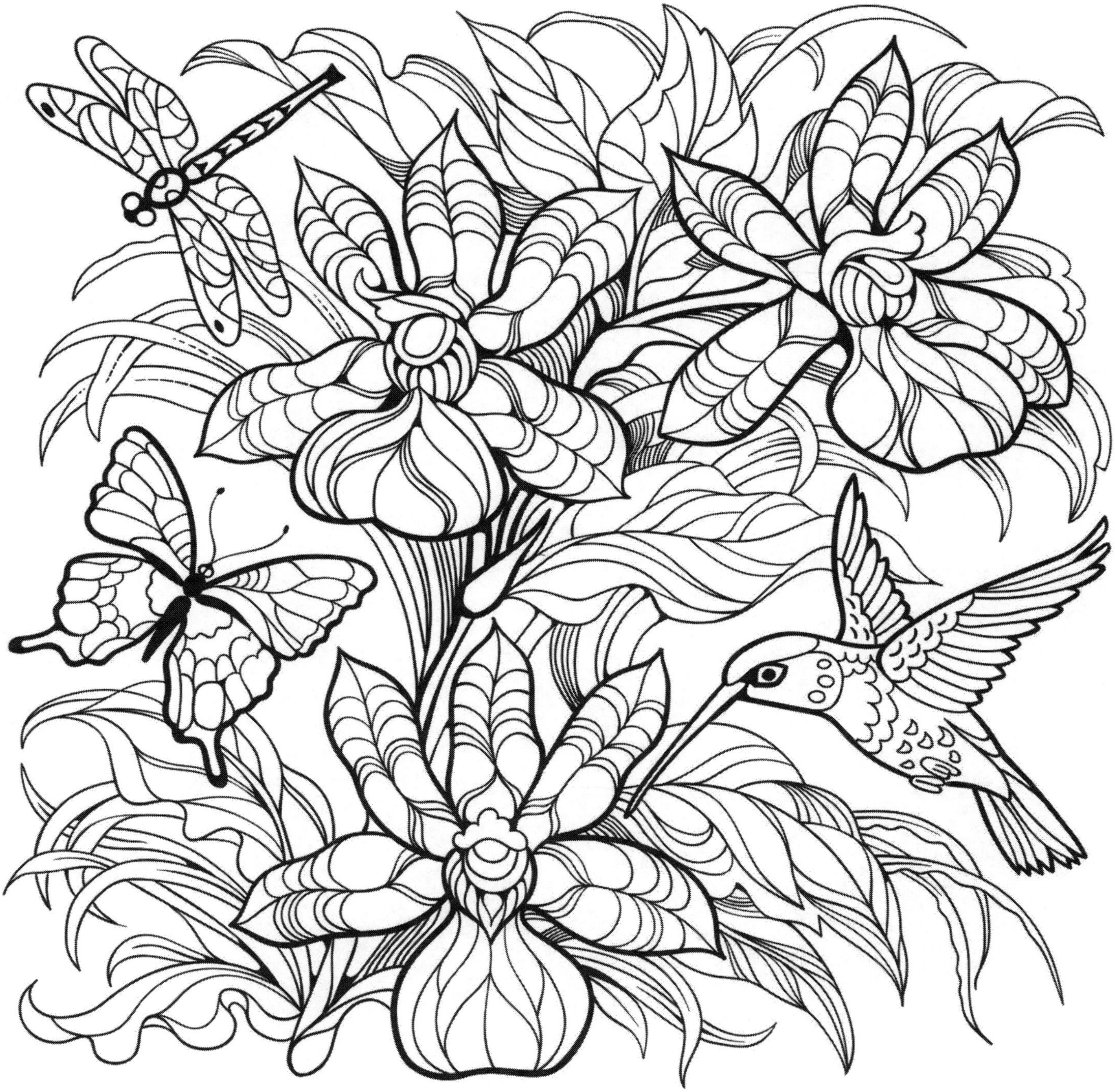

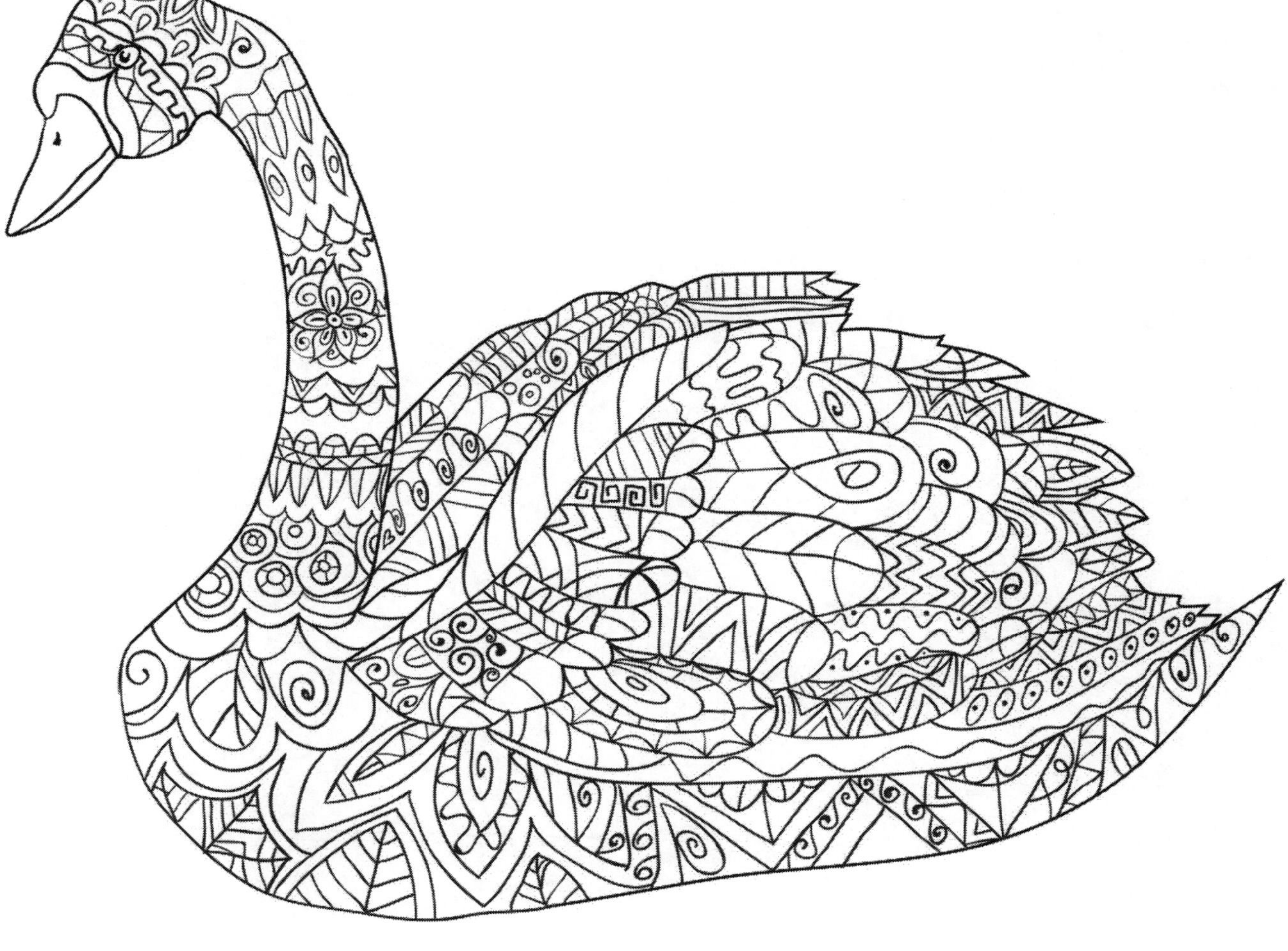

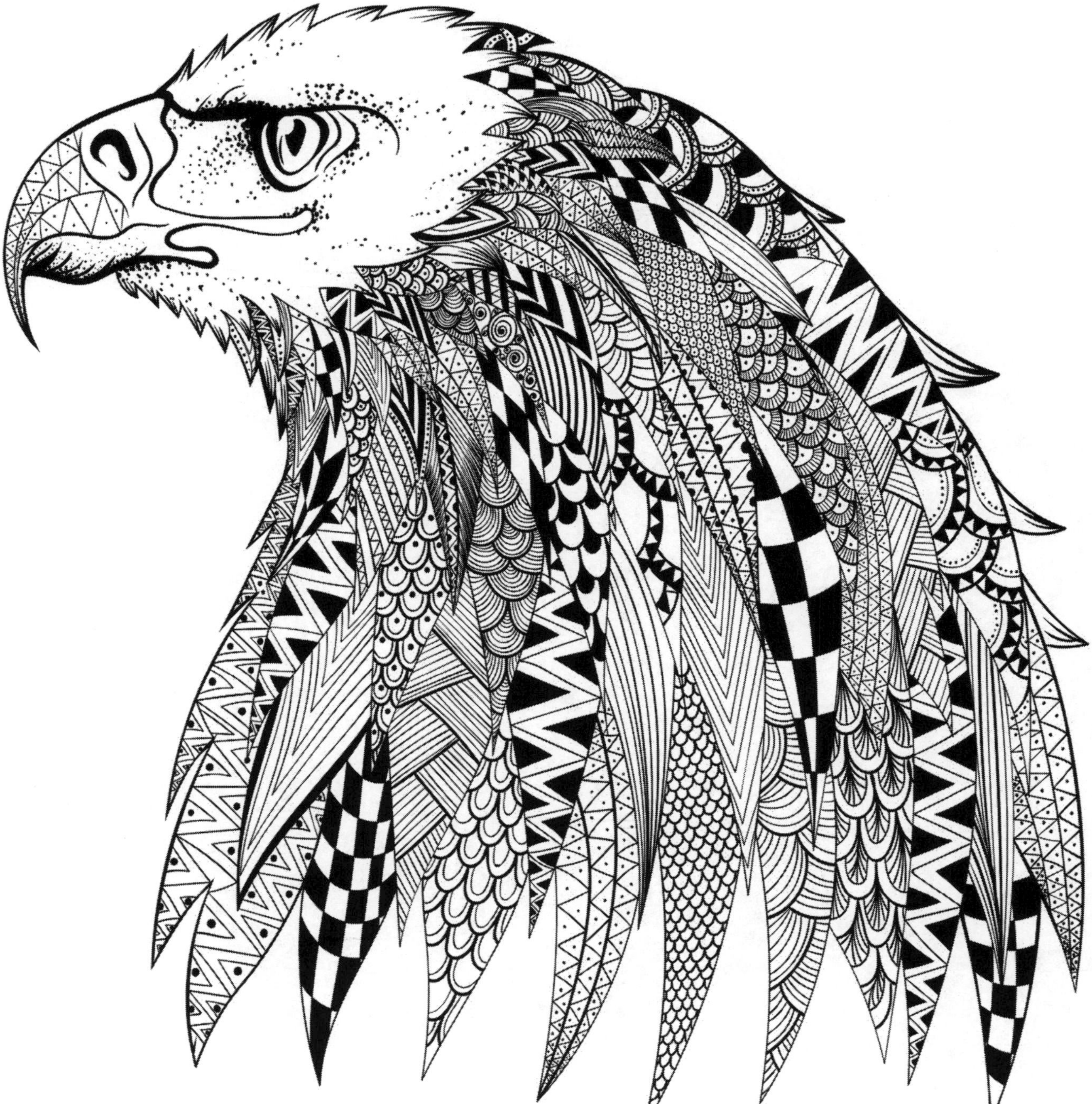

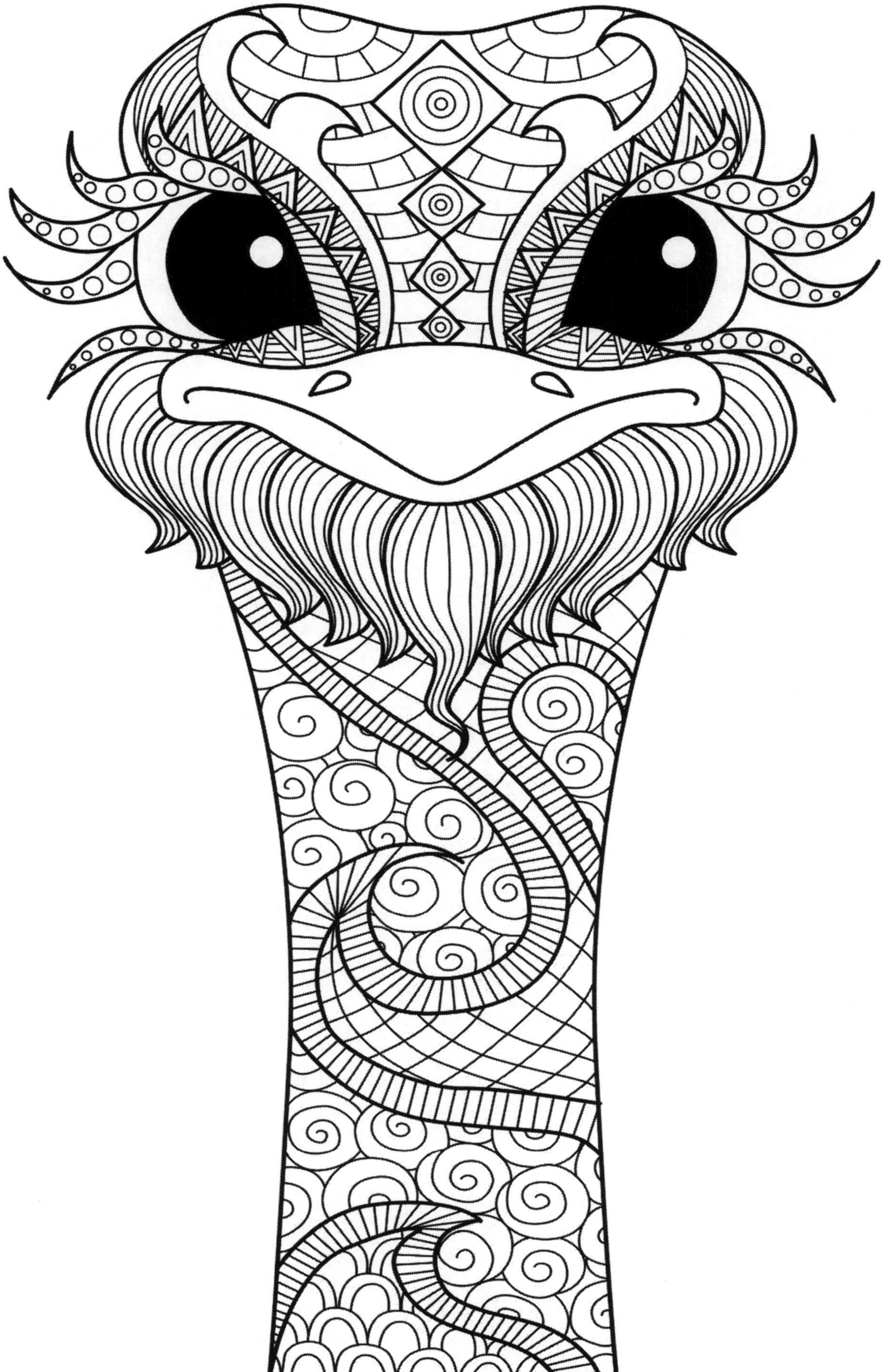

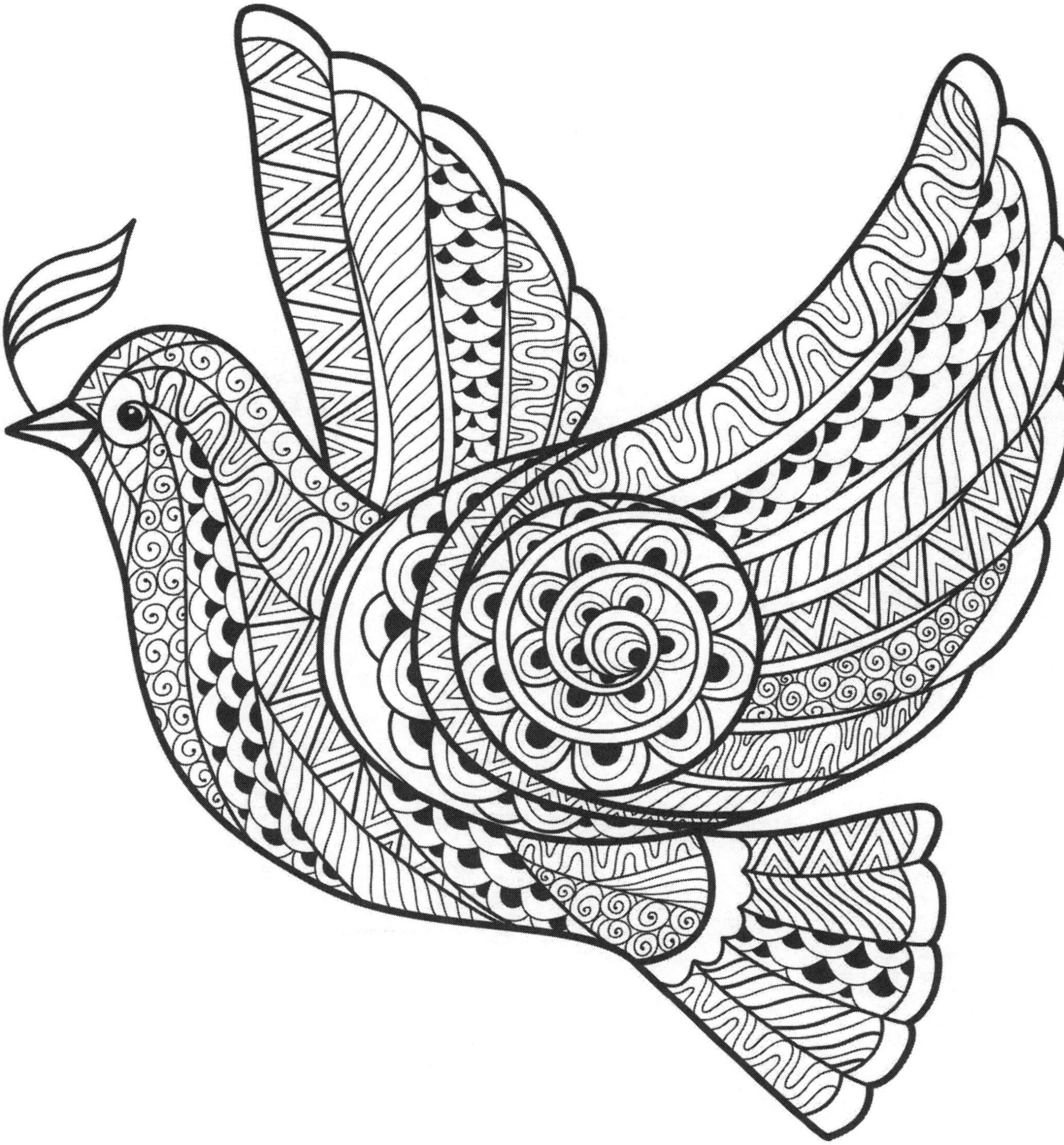

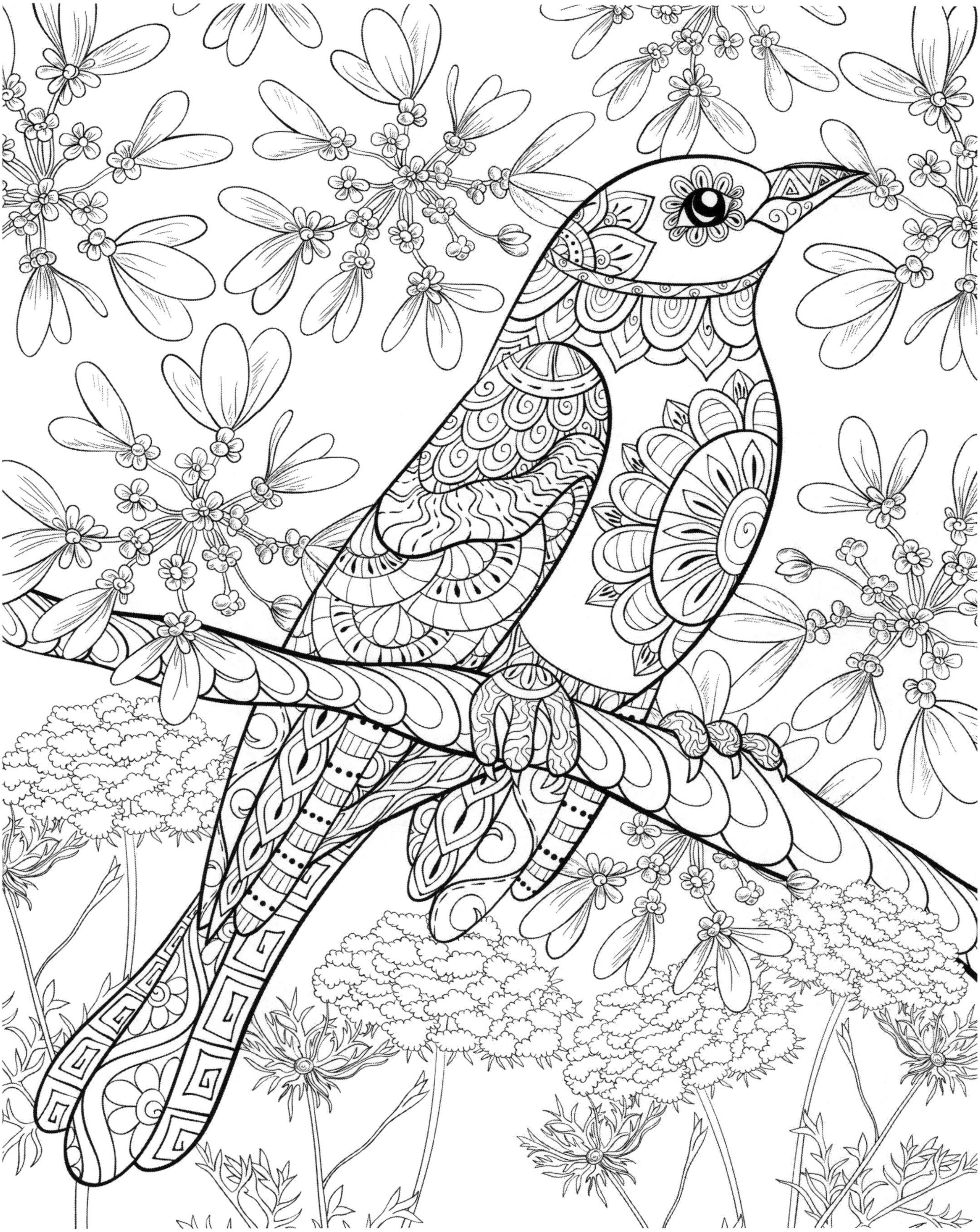

54524229R00062

Made in the USA
San Bernardino,
CA